the facebook book

THIS BOOK IS A WORK OF FICTION, A PARODY.
Neither Mark Zuckerberg nor Facebook has in any way
sponsored, approved, endorsed, or authorized this book.
Any similarities to persons, living or dead, or to any
existing entities or companies are purely coincidental.

Editor: Aiah R. Wieder
Designer: Alissa Faden
Production Manager: Jacquie Poirier

Library of Congress Cataloging-in-Publication Data

Atwan, Greg, 1983–
  The Facebook book / by Greg Atwan & Evan Lushing ; illustrated by
Aurora Andrews.
      p. cm.
  ISBN 978-0-8109-9557-4 (pbk.)
  1. Facebook—Parodies, imitations, etc. I. Lushing, Evan, 1981– II.
Andrews, Aurora, 1984– III. Title.

  PN6231.F24A89 2008
  006.7—dc22

                         2007044463

Published in 2008 by Abrams Image, an imprint of Harry N. Abrams, Inc.

Printed and bound in the United States
10 9 8 7 6 5 4 3 2 1

HNA ▮▮▮▮▮
harry n. abrams, inc.
a subsidiary of La Martinière Groupe

115 West 18th Street
New York, NY 10011
www.hnabooks.com

the facebook book

{ *a satirical* }
{ *companion* }

BY GREG ATWAN AND EVAN LUSHING

ILLUSTRATED BY AURORA ANDREWS

ABRAMS IMAGE
NEW YORK

contents

Dear Reader,

You might be wondering why I, Mark Zuckerberg, the youngest CEO in North America (Gurdayal Patel, 14, I'm gunning for you), would take the time out of my day to write an introduction to this, a dead-tree book. After all, when man invented fire, did he continue to eat raw meat? When the Zuck bestowed Facebook upon the citizenry, did they continue to use Friendster? The arrow of progress is diamond-tipped and lightning-quick, and it cannot be stopped by man, beast, or firewall . . . or an actual wall of fire, for that matter. So I counsel you, dear reader, to put down this molded tome (overweight at 8 ounces), jog to the nearest hotspot, and read a blog or Drudge Report or a Google Map. Better yet, sign on to Facebook and send some gifts. We got this great new one that's a Rubik's Cube with your friends' faces on it. A steal at $1.75.

But to answer your question. Why did I contribute my time to this fruitless venture? I could have programmed three apps and poked a whole high school in the time it's taking me to write this (FYI: I'm just a really slow writer; those are not simple tasks). There is actually a very good reason, beyond the fact that Greg and Evan agreed not to include screenshots of FaceMash if I introduced their book. That reason is this: Facebook is not just a facebook. It's not just the most popular website for collegians. It's not just in the name of the second most popular MIT major ("Facebook Studies"). . . . It's a way of perceiving reality. Hyperbole? Hubris? Insanity? Don't think so. I'm quoting a study done by actual professors and scientists at an accredited institution. The same guys behind Super-Duper String Theory.

What I'm trying to get at is this: When the paradigm is shifted, some people (old people) can feel left out. With the advent of rock 'n' roll in the sixties of the previous century, a cappella and zydeco were forced to retreat to regional festivals and liberal arts campuses. Thusly, the march of progress. For those of you left getting your news via the application of graphite depositions to cellulose, or nautical semaphore, I offer you this book, a good old-timey folio like mama used to read. Look and feel it now, cozy and firm in your hands. Nary a virus or spammer to be found. The content won't update, no matter how stale it gets. Read at your leisure with any available light source, including (but not limited to) gas lamp. Will you enjoy it? No idea. Never read it. But you'll sure learn about what you're missing. And who wouldn't pay a couple of Indian Head nickels for that!

Sincerely,

The Zuck, CEO

A Key to Special Features

TIMELINES

CHECKLISTS ✔

LETTERS & EMAILS ✉

FIRST-PERSON

MORALIST SAYS

FUTURIST SAYS

CONFUCIUS SAYS

ECONOMIST EXPLAINS

TIPSTER SAYS

facebook
is huge

friend
(n) a person bonded to another on Facebook
(v) to add as a friend (using Facebook)

—*Merriam-Webster's Dictionary*, 2093 edition

How Huge Is Huge?

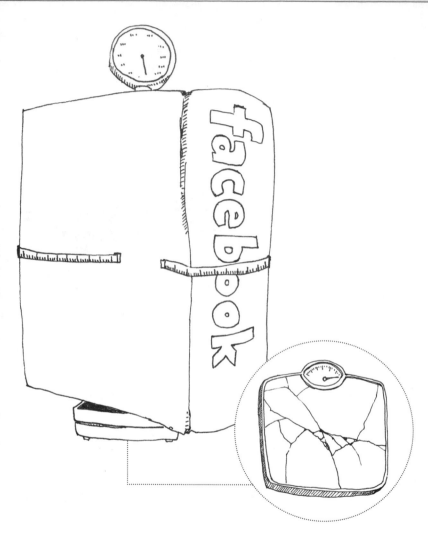

You've heard the stats: 60 million users, 10,000 registrations a day, most popular site for people under twenty-five, least popular site for neo-Nazis. But stats are the poor man's words. How big is Facebook really?

FACEBOOK IS

- Justin Timberlake performs at your high school big.
- the iPod's share of the MP3-player market big.
- the Dalai Lama's preeminence over other lamas big.
- Google big.

IF FACEBOOK WERE

- a Vegas casino, all of its slot machines would be those jumbo ones you see in the lobby.
- an NBA player, it would actually be fairly unskilled because it could dominate on size alone.
- a Monopoly token, it would be the anvil stacked on the dog.
- a store, it would be a Wal-Mart with a McDonald's sub-store.

What's the last big movie you can think of? It involved dwarves and Wagner, right? Didn't exactly alter the customs of socializing, now did it? What about the last big personal transportation device? Remember, the one that was supposed to be a rocket-pack but ended up being a roller skate with a pole? Didn't quite revolutionize *flirting*. And what about the last big Supreme Court decision? The one about habeas corpus on international territory governed by a military agency. Wow. That didn't even warrant a shout-out in *Newsweek*.

FACEBOOK IS AS BIG AS IT GETS

Can you think of something bigger than changing the nature of *friendship*—an institution that's literally been around since before the Masons? But that's not all Facebook has changed.

Procrastination: Practically invented the concept of power procrastination, and popularized the procrast-a-break and procrasti-contemplation.

Television habits: Killed off the reality-TV fad with a dose of actual reality (although MTV kept pace with *The Real World: Facebook*).

Laziness: It's been legitimized by its frequent depiction on the Book.

THE VICTORIAN FACEBOOK

Friend-related trivia games

Portrait photography

Offtrack betting (anticipated in 2009)

A BRIEF FACEBOOK PREHISTORY

10,000 BC

Zoologists report that a tribe of Bonobos in eastern Cameroon assign each individual a large stone ("profile") in the middle of a camp, on which other members of the tribe may leave either twigs ("friend requests") or excrement ("graffiti").

292 AD

A certain Mayan inscription from the Yaxhá temple includes the glyph for "face" immediately before the one for "scroll." Mesoamerican experts dispute whether the phrase refers to an early social directory or to a guy who had information about the year's grain harvest tattooed on his forehead.

1886 AD

A now-obscure Victorian amateur scientist, Zebadiah Henry (later Lord Trowbutter), achieved brief fame with the Tele-Electrical Facial Exposition Machine. Using three steam engines, a primitive current, and a team of African zebras, the device would take a name in Morse code and, several hours later, return an image of the subject by an eminent portraitist, along with some vital information. The profile was similar to today's, with some minor differences: Instead of networks there were peerages, and instead of relationship status there was knighthood status. Queen Victoria herself attempted to "friend" President Garfield but instead caused a furor when she accidentally propositioned a Kentucky moonshiner named Gurfield. The Machine was abandoned almost immediately, but Gurfield never stopped sending the Queen messages.

FACEBOOK VS. MYSPACE

By the time you're reading this, Facebook has thoroughly deposed MySpace for the social-network crown. Just as Victoria Beckham vanquished Posh Spice, MySpace has slunk off into kitschy oblivion, the subject only of VH1 reminiscences. Truthfully, it wasn't that close a match. If Facebook is the tony washroom at an exclusive country club, MySpace was a highway rest stop. Its chaotic Web 1.0 aesthetic appealed to people who spend a lot of time looking at Frank Zappa album covers. As a result, it was so overrun with weirdos, noobs, gangbangers, and twelve-year-olds that it offered nothing to even the marginally hip.

Which is to say: If you still have a MySpace account in the post-Facebook age, you are probably one or more of the following:

- a porn star
- a porn star's assistant
- a self-repped creative type
- a grungy blogger
- a Satanist
- a member of a Grateful Dead tribute band
- a founder of a Facebook also-ran
- a flashmob aficionado
- a European porn star
- a stadium magician
- a substitute teacher
- a pinballer
- a suburban musician
- a lounge type

A GRUNGY BLOGGER

MILESTONE HEADLINES IN FACEBOOK'S HISTORY:

The Times
Facebook: Kind of a Big Deal

Harvard Students Can't Socialize in Real World, Try Online
Ivy-League dweebs build themselves virtual tree house
The Boston Globe (2/23/04)

Missing Teen Found in Facebook Group
Online discovery is "good enough," parents say
San Francisco Chronicle (3/8/05)

Southern Values Politician Outed on Facebook
Congressman says by "interested in men" he meant as voters
The Atlanta Journal-Constitution (7/15/05)

Facebook a Decadent Western Evil
American gluttons squander harvesting time in false friendship ritual
North Korean State News Service (9/21/06)

Kim Jong Il Has Most Facebook Friends Ever
Exalted Dear Leader is poked almost constantly
North Korean State News Service (10/31/06)

Friendster Founder Starts Facebook Profile
Entrepreneur "just not meeting any hot girls anymore"
Chicago Tribune (5/7/07)

Le Monde

Facebook, J'Accuse

Mark Zuckerberg Does It Again, Invents Game to Replace Chess
Modest boy genius got idea for Backwards-Pawn from a dream
Facebook Internal Newsletter (1/8/08)

FACEBOOK POPULARITY CHART

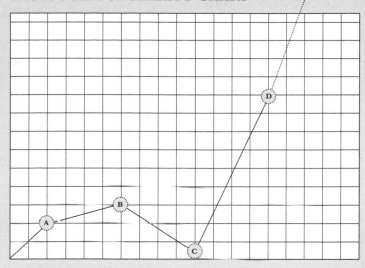

(A) Early Days
Population equal to: Western Nebraska; die-hard fans of the Washington Nationals; a typical kibbutz

(B) The Word Gets Out
Population equal to: The Mid-Atlantic states; people who have heard of the Rolling Stones; doctors and lawyers

(C) A Substantial Dip
This was on 7/7/07, when America's youth pledged not to use the Internet for a day in solidarity with the environment

(D) Current Levels
Population equal to: South America; people who aren't very good at math; workers

(E) The Future?
Population equal to: Everyone, including pets and ghosts

FACEBOOK'S INDEX

83 Number of A-list celebrities with Facebook profiles

24,332 Number of B- and C-list celebrities with MySpace profiles

53 Minimum number of friends a high-school girl must have on the Book not to be considered a social outcast

28 Percentage of Facebook users who list a book they've never even read as one of their favorite books of all time

5 Percentage of Facebook users who misattribute "I'd rather die enormous than live dormant" to Shakespeare

8 Percentage of Facebook users who misattribute "let slip the dogz of war" to Jay-Z

1 Number of former U.S. presidents who have a secret profile on Facebook modeled after a character from *Gossip Girl*

0 Number of popes on Facebook

18 Average number of hours high-school students reported last year as "community service" that were actually spent looking at the profiles of people they considered losers

0.02 Percentage of members who claim they came up with the idea for Facebook first

104 Number of profiles that are just proxies for sociology PhD candidates writing their dissertations on "hooking up in the postcolonial world"

90 Number of hours per week Team Facebook spends responding to requests from members for a feature that allows them to see who visited their profile without letting others know whose profiles they've visited

17 Number of confirmed octogenarians who have Facebook profiles

24 Average age of Team Facebook employees, excluding lobbyists and defense department coordinators

5 Percentage increase in Philadelphia tourism after Shia LaBeouf befriended the Liberty Bell profile

891 Number of children who could be fed by the cupcake gifts given out on the Book per month, if the cupcakes were real and fortified with essential vitamins

31 Percentage of photo albums titled "Spring Break in Prague" that were actually taken in Budapest

15 Percentage of members who claim their hometown is Los Angeles whose real hometown is either Encino or the Netherlands

41 Number of fetuses that have "started" a profile

209 Number of patent applications the USPO received last year for drinking games that incorporated the Book as a major element

6 Number of hermaphrodites with both male and female profiles

100 Percentage of Nobel Prize-winning economists who believe Facebook will lead to the eventual downfall of the paperback facebook industry

5 Length in minutes a mother, on average, will confusedly search for her son or daughter's profile on fakebook.com

11 Percentage of U.S. farmers on the Book

93 Percentage of U.S. pharmers on the Book

65,000 Length in words of the profile of Richard Posner, notoriously long-winded jurist

1,440 Weight in pounds of Team Facebook's top secret Project Delta (a wind-powered Internet server)

1 billion
Number of children who will never know a world without Facebook

FASCINATING RATIOS

1:6 Ratio of sketchy to nonsketchy people on Facebook

7:1 Ratio on the Internet at large

1:1 Ratio of philosophers to philanderers

3:2 Ratio of metrosexuals to lipstick lesbians

2:3 Ratio of lipstick lesbians to metrosexuals

THE FACEBOOK ALSO-RANS

KarmaHog: A Hindu-inflected network that allowed users to profile both their current life-form and up to six previous incarnations. Shut down after too many people erroneously claimed to have been Jim Morrison. [*FAILED: October 2006*]

Gary's Original Facebook: Gary Greenburg claims to have invented a website exactly like Facebook a few weeks before Zuckerberg, but of course it's better because it lets you type in italics, too. The same Gary of Gary's Original Google and Gary's Awesome Autoparts. [*FAILED: December 2006*]

Faceboooooooook: A business major at Babson tried to capitalize on typing errors. (URLs with up to 8 o's are owned by the Team.) Only ever got traffic from people looking for Faceboooooooooo, an angry blog about plastic surgery. [*FAILED: February 2007*]

FriendBook: Not a website per se, but an urban youth group dedicated to bringing kids together over a shared interest in books. Declined in popularity after vandals ripped all the pop-ups out of the pop-up books. [*FAILED: October 2007*]

FacelessBook: A conceptual Facebook that de-emphasized physical appearance. You were forbidden from using a photo of your face as a profile picture. But you could easily get around this by taking a photo of a photo of your face. [*FAILED: January 2008*]

Friendster: The thing before MySpace. Like Billy Crystal, still around only out of perverse nostalgia. Ugly, full of grad students in the humanities, and buggier than a log in a swamp. [*WILL FAIL: September 2008*]

LinkedIn: Remember those young-adult books you read to feel as smart as a regular adult? But they were really just kids' books with no pictures? The young people on this site forget that the old people who can advance their careers think the Internet and PlayStation 2 are the same thing. [*WILL FAIL: mid-2009*]

Orkut: Actually quite popular, but only in South America. Google purchased it for the same reason that Angelina Jolie adopts babies from exotic continents: good cocktail conversation. [*WILL FAIL: after the next coup in Brazil or Mountain View*]

FRIENDSHIP IS DIFFERENT WITH FACEBOOK

Sure, people made friends before Facebook, but how? Sock hops? Church socials? Town squares? Cousins? Village Olympics? School?

Before Facebook making friends involved a lot of knickknacks. You had your bracelet buddies, pinned pals, brooch bros, and chewing-gum chums. You gave your friend a thing, your friend gave you a similar thing in return, and you were officially friended. (In Appalachian country, you also sealed a document with red wax.) Facebook takes this druidic rite and cyberizes it. When a friendship is created on the Book, the names are inscribed on a page of the great Friendship Book, which is kept safe in the basement of Facebook HQ. When a friendship is broken off, the page is ceremoniously burned. This process became laborious when Facebook passed the million-user mark. Now they do the whole thing with flammable Post-it notes.

FRIENDSHIP BEFORE AND AFTER FACEBOOK IS LIKE REGULAR DEFINITION TELEVISION AND HDTV. AT FIRST IT'S TOO MUCH INFORMATION . . . BUT THEN YOU REALIZE IT'S THE UGLY DETAILS THAT MAKE YOU FEEL BETTER ABOUT YOURSELF.

Before Facebook how did we find out what our friends were up to? None of the historians and archivists we interviewed could remember. The only guy who had the slightest recollection was a Ulysses S. Grant impersonator:

> **Q.** *How do you find out what your friends are doing?*
>
> **A.** Why, I see them every day at the local alehouse.

Q. *But what about your friends who don't live nearby? Like friends from high school.*

A. Dead. All dead from the war. . . . A few just maimed beyond recognition.

Before Facebook how did we know who had the most friends? In prison, it's the guy with the most teardrop tattoos. In grade school, the kid with the most Halloween candy year-round. In the corporate world, it's the tallest guy (who is not bald). But these are just rules of thumb. One's true friend count was always as nebulous as that stain on your futon.

Before Facebook you could never really end a friendship, either. Not for good and certain. Not without making a big scene in the cafeteria in which mothers and chastities were impugned. Dean Martin famously tried to end his friendship with Jerry Lewis by sending a fake hit man to kill the comedian. But that just gave Jerry the idea for his movie *What a Guy!*

On Facebook, you're either friends or you're not. Sure, there are Top Friends, Friend Groups, and dismissive Details, but in the end, membership on your profile is binary. You can't shrug someone off by telling everyone he's your cousin from Kentucky, and you can't pretend you forgot a random hookup's name and/ or facial features. Friend, or not friend.

Before Facebook you had to make your own Book. Bill Clinton kept a shoebox filled with index cards of his friends. Despite his prodigious memory, he couldn't quite remember every municipal tax assessor and suzie-floozy who crossed his path. Some would say that shoebox won Bill the White House. Others would argue it was his shoebox filled with illegal political donations that did it.

The last big thing to happen to friendship was the mid-90s flagship sitcom *Friends*. It proved against all wisdom that men and women could have a deep, rewarding friendship without sex. Before that, it was the buddy-comedy trend of the mid-80s (*48 Hours, Stakeout, Armed and Dangerous*, et al.), which proved that a cop and a criminal could have a deep, rewarding friendship without all that much sex.

A REJECTED FACEBOOK RESUME

THIS WAS THE NAME OF MY PEDIATRICIAN. HE HAD OILY FINGERS

Martin Schlosser
231 Audley St.
Poway, California

ISN'T BLINK 182 FROM THERE?

- DOESN'T EVEN HAVE A WIKIPEDIA PAGE

High School: Earl A. Vandermullen High

College: Stanford, BA 2006

OOOH! STANFORD! HARVARD 2.0, ALMA MATER OF TED KOPPEL. FEEDER SCHOOL TO SUCCESS. SAVE IT FOR THE IN-LAWS.

GPA/SAT score: 3.75/2250

THOSE ARE MY MYSPACE NUMBERS

Honors and Activities:
Google Labs Design Award, Special Recognition
Tutor, Leg-Up in Math Program Member, Phi Beta
Tau, Honors Society, Film Club

I'M PRETTY SURE THAT'S JUST A PARTICIPATION PRIZE. YOU KNOW, LIKE THE CROWN YOU GET AT BURGER KING EVEN WHEN IT'S NOT YOUR BIRTHDAY.

Work History:
Summer 2004, National Security Agency
internship; Summer 2005, Xerox Park internship;
Summer 2006, IBM Youth Scholars; the Microsoft
Challenge

OH, DID YOU GO TO SPACE CAMP TOO?

Computer Languages: C/C++, Java, Python,
Lisp, Scheme, Maple

WHY DOESN'T HE JUST LIST ELVISH? NERD.

PASS

NOTE: CHECKED HIS FACEBOOK PROFILE. SOULLESS, AND HIS CHOICE OF APPS IS HAPHAZARD. LIKE A QUARTERBACK ABOUT TO GET RUSHED.

THIS WAS THE NAME OF MY PEDIATRICIAN. HE HAD OILY ——— FINGERS

...Audley St.
...oway, California

DOESN'T EVEN HAVE A WIKIPEDIA PAGE

ISN'T BLINK 182 FROM THERE?

——— OOOH! STANFORD! HARVARD 2.0, ALMA MATER OF TED KOPPEL. FEEDER SCHOOL TO SUCCESS. SAVE IT FOR THE IN-LAWS.

THOSE ARE MY MYSPACE NUMBERS

Math Program Member, Phi Beta
...iety, Film Club

I'M PRETTY SURE THAT'S JUST A PARTICIPATION PRIZE. YOU KNOW, LIKE THE CROWN YOU GET AT BURGER KING EVEN WHEN ITS NOT YOUR BIRTHDAY.

OH, DID YOU GO TO SPACE CAMP TOO?

WHY DOESN'T HE JUST LIST ELVISH? NERD.

: CHECKED HIS FACEBOOK PROFILE. SOULLESS, AND HIS CHOICE OF APPS IS HAPHAZARD. LIKE A QUARTERBACK ABOUT TO GET RUSHED.

WORKING AT FACEBOOK

The Facebook Job Interview

Q. *We don't have much time, so let's get started. I only have one question for you: What can you bring to Facebook that we don't already have? Keep in mind that we already have three Turing Award–winning computer scientists and a party van. Were you going to say party van? Because we could use a slightly larger party van.*

A. I was the top of my class at CalTech and I worked every summer at Google's advanced research lab.

Q. *I'm going to stop you right there. Can you drive a party van? I don't mean do you have a specific license to drive one, just in general would you feel comfortable driving a party van? Because it's a lot more fun to ride in a party van than it is to drive one, and people haven't been as eager to volunteer since the CFO installed a Wii back there.*

A. I guess I could drive it—

Q. *Miniature golf. Do you play and, more importantly, do you know how to get to the one off Route 286? That's where we take the party van primarily. I guess you could look it up on Google Maps. It's called "A Hole in Fun." Do you know how to use Google Maps? I've heard it's fairly straightforward.*

A. Look, I graduated summa in computer science—

Q. *Zuckerberg doesn't like to lose, but he also doesn't like to win too easily. There's an art to this miniature golf thing. I say beat him on the castle and the dinosaur up front, and let him win the rest. The winner gets to ride shotgun on the way back. Did I mention that?*

A. No.

Q. *It's arguably the most prestigious prize you can win playing for Team Facebook, besides stock options. You win those on a per-hole basis. I've got like ten thousand, but I'm pretty good. I've got a system.*

A. . . .

Q. *The system is you overshoot the hole by like a foot. Sounds simple, I know. But a lot of these computer geeks are too conservative, they want to get it precisely in the hole. But that's not how you win in golf or life. You've got to overshoot your dreams, like Anna Nicole did.*

A BUSINESS SCHOOL PROFESSOR
TALKS ABOUT FACEBOOK

Q. *So Facebook is a pretty great business model, right?*

A. Selling moustache wax in Brooklyn is a pretty great business model. Facebook is an effing great business model. We spend most of class fantasizing about working there.

Q. *But isn't there a chance Zuckerberg just got lucky? I mean the Internet is still a crazy place—*

A. Did Beethoven get lucky? Did Churchill get lucky? Did that guy who won Powerball twice get lucky? To quote a great orator and statesman, "Luck is for lame-o's."

Q. *What can we learn from Facebook, business-wise?*

A. Truthfully, not much. You could spend all day watching Federer serve, but it ain't gonna make you better. In fact, you'll probably get worse because of the intimidation factor. I tell my students: Stay away from the Internet. The game is over. Facebook won, and the runner-up prize is a warm bucket of ConnectU-stew.

Q. *Are you on Facebook?*

A. God, no. I'm a total Twitter-twit.

profile of a profile

In the same way that water doesn't seem to taste like anything, Facebook doesn't seem to have much of a design style. But drink polluted water or visit MySpace some time, and you'll realize art is sometimes the trees you don't paint.

ABSENCE IS PRESENCE. —— *A truant we once knew*

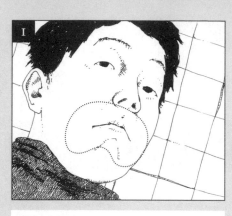

1

Complete the Profile

TO TEST YOUR KNOWLEDGE OF FACEBOOK CULTURE, WE'VE SELECTED PROFILES FROM ACTUAL BOOKSTERS AND DELETED SOME OF THEIR INFO. CAN YOU FILL IN THE BLANKS?

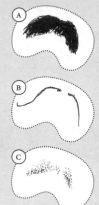

I

YOUR ANSWER:

2

YOUR ANSWER:

3

A

FRIEND
WHORE

B

SAVING MYSELF
FOR MARRIAGE
OR TONIGHT
(WHICHEVER
COMES FIRST)

C

I guess
I support
Obama

YOUR ANSWER:

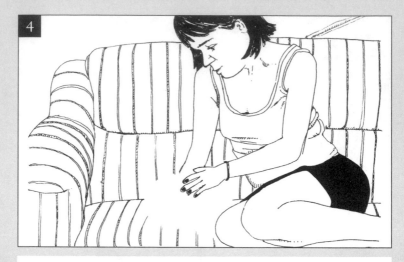

YOUR ANSWER:

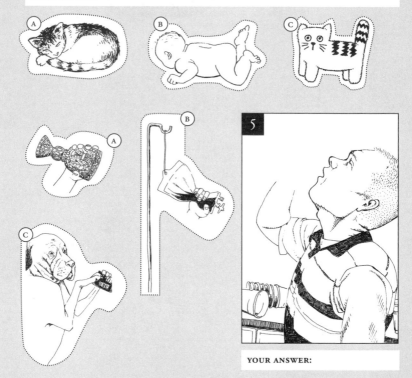

YOUR ANSWER:

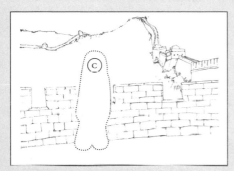

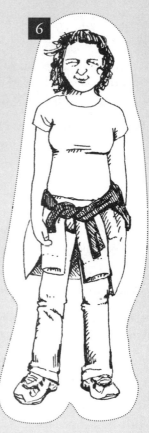

YOUR ANSWER:

Favorite Movies: Lord of the Rings 1, _____, Lord of the Rings 3, that 70s TV movie cartoon of The Hobbit

Favorite Books: College Humor's Guide To Making a(n) _____ of Yourself on the Web (Grad School Edition)

Contact:
Mobile   17.555.2583

Groups:
(*fill in the blank with one word to form the name of a real Facebook Group*)

For every ten people who join this group I'll _____ a lonely frosh

The Chuck Norris Ultra-Fan Club, _____ Dakota Chapter

Appreciation Society for the Saxophonist in Dave Matthews _____

If this group gets five thousand members I'll shave off my _____ with _____ a in front of the whole _____

Race for awareness of the horrible little-known disease which everyone MUST hear about called _____

Legalize Marijuana . . . or at the very least let us smoke it out of _____

I slept with Professor _____ and all I got was a slightly higher GPA at Middlebury

High School Students Whose Favorite Wilson Brother is _____ Wilson

I WAS SO HIGH WHEN I MADE THIS PROFILE

facebook

I FORGOT MY NAME Jesus Christ, I literally forgot my name.

Sex:	Male
Interested In:	Women
Address:	the universe

Personal Information

Favorite Movies: Oh man I just saw the craziest YouTube video, there was this squirrel and cat fighting, and Star Wars kid was there dancing on a treadmill.

Favorite Books: my friend's blog, the graphic novelization of Heroes (web-only)

Favorite Music: aw dip aw dip aw dip I just spilled bong water on the keyboard and I was gonna water my "plants" with that

Activities: I wonder if I pour Fritos on it will their nacho-y composition absorb it.

Interests: it worked but now that cat that looks like Giuliani is licking it

About Me: What if facebook is the real world and the real world is actually facebook, and wars are programming bugs and Zuckerberg is the dream-master. Does that mean if I defriend someone they die?

James Stoner   Margaret Stonewell

The Wall

 I FORGOT MY NAME wrote (August 27, 2006):
I also accidentally wrote on my real wall

REJECTED PROFILE LAYOUT IDEAS:

In that fantastical opium dream in which Zuckerberg conceived of the Book, he came up with a number of design styles. To his great good fortune, he chose the last one: clean. Here are the others, which we found scribbled on graph paper in a Harvard dumpster.

The MC Escher: Looks the same if you rotate your monitor 90 degrees; the beer bong gift flows uphill; your profile pic morphs gradually over time into a fish.

The Frank Gehry: To be designed on commission by Frank's firm: Imagine looking at your computer screen through a melted kaleidoscope while an oboe plays in the distance.

The 8-bit Nintendo: Retro, big pixels; a vine grows to the top of your screen, where a cloud-gremlin throws down pictures of your friends.

The All-Text: Nothing but text, like DOS or UNIX; emoticons are also forbidden.

The Virtual Facebook: Digitized images of a paperback Facebook; for added realism, the pages occasionally stick together and fray, and can only be repaired by purchasing the Glue Gizmo.

The Matrix: Nothing to do with Neo and bondage, just a spreadsheet with your friends' names neatly alphabetized or sorted according to exoticness.

The Sandbox: Total freedom to design your profile page—but only using the spray-can tool.

The Bloomberg: Modeled after the luxury mayor's financial wiz-box, all your friends' names are abbreviated and charts represent their fluctuating social prominence.

The Rothko: Boxes within boxes; no text; color-coded.

The New Yorker: Laid out like the magazine: austere, sophisticated, and cartoony.

INTERVIEW: CHIEF FACEBOOK DESIGNER

Q. *Where did you work before joining Team Facebook?*

A. I freelanced. A lot of gigs doing cereal boxes and rich kids' blogs. I also drove a truck in *Second Life*.

Q. *Who are your inspirations?*

A. Gaia. Mother Nature. Trees. Rodents. Fog. Inspiration is everywhere. Look around. Right there—a spider. My next layout will have eight boxes.

Q. *How important do you think design is to Facebook's success?*

A. As important as showmanship is to a rapper.

Q. *What are the new trends you see in Web design?*

A. I must take issue with your phrasing. I do not design for the Web: I design for the soul. If the Internet didn't exist, Facebook could be fashioned out of playing cards and cheese and it would be exactly as good. But to answer your question, I see a pop-up window renaissance in the near future.

Q. *Describe Facebook's design philosophy in a word.*

A. Ultraminimalistication.

Q. *Where do you see Facebook in ten years?*

A. On an IMAX screen in Times Square. It will be Coke and the *New York Times* rolled into one.

Q. *Who are your rivals in the design world?*

A. My biggest rival is my yesterday-self. My second biggest rival is my day-before-yesterday-self. Design is a mountain which must be climbed without sherpas or shoes. The only thing I'm focused on is the rocky crag in front of me—the face of Don Porter, my boss.

Q. *Do you like the layouts of any other websites?*

A. There's a Swedish furniture maker whose website has no edges. I keep it in my Del.icio.us folder.

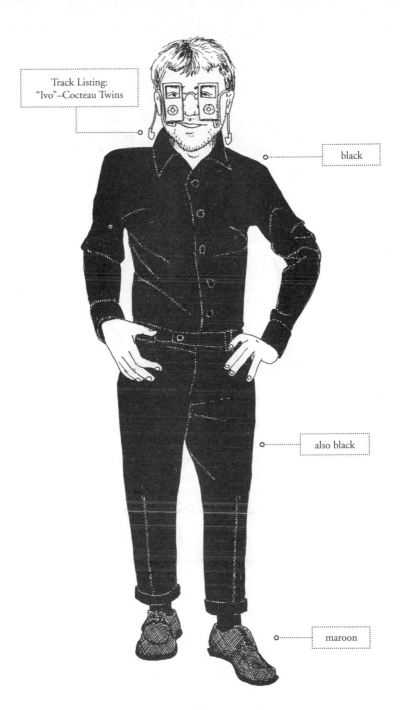

Track Listing:
"Ivo"–Cocteau Twins

black

also black

maroon

FAVORITE MOVIES

You can't really brag about having seen a movie. Not even some-thing Czech. Not even something with Chris Kattan. There's no cinematic equivalent to reading *War and Peace*. And no one will get into a bar fight with you over your taste in early Eddie Murphy showcase pieces either. Movies are just for fun. But this is Facebook, so you better be having all different kinds of fun.

From each category choose one film.

Black-and-White Classic: *Casablanca* is fine, but clichéd; choose another Bogart, like *The Maltese Falcon* or *Bogart Remembers Bogart*. Similarly, *Roman Holiday* over *Breakfast at Tiffany's* over the *Breakfast at Tiffany's* music video.

Movie That Came Out Within the Last Year: Safe choice is the fourth-highest-grossing film of the summer or the latest aw-shucks-Steve-Carell-will-end-up-okay romp.

Something Really Deep: *Donnie Darko*, *Mulholland Dr.*, or *Koyaanisqatsi*, the Phillip Glass allegory that was basically a screen saver with a soundtrack.

Obscure Foreign Film: Avoid the low-hanging fruit of popular imports like *Y tu mamá también* or *Police Academy 7: Mission to Moscow*. A deep cut says, "I turn off the subtitles on the DVD."

Guilty Pleasure: Even Emeril eats cookie dough now and then. Anything with Chevy Chase is automatically frosted enough; early Olsen Twins also, excluding their *Scared Straight* work.

Comfort Film: A place to show your roots. *Fried Green Tomatoes* if your mother cooked a lot; *The Sandlot* if you had a fat, sandy-haired friend; and *The Goonies* if you rode your bike all over town.

Surprise Choice: Guys, pick a cheesy romantic comedy (*Notting Hill*, *The Princess Diaries*). Girls, pick something erotic and nasty (*Cruel Intentions*, *The Princess Diaries*).

FAVORITE MUSIC

The Facebook generation was previously the Napster generation and, as a result, downloaded a lot of misattributed songs. Before you declare a favorite artist, keep in mind:

- Bob Dylan didn't write "Stuck in the Middle with You."
- Jimmy Buffet didn't write "Escape (The Piña Colada Song)."
- Dave Matthews Band didn't write "Uncle John's Band."
- Green Day didn't write "Heroin" or "Cocaine."
- Bruce Springsteen didn't write "Back in the USSR."
- Kelly Clarkson didn't write any of her songs.

FAVORITE TV SHOWS

The Favorite TV Shows field is your opportunity for vivid self-expression. Here are just a few of the many colors available to you on the televisional palette:

- The rich, sexual aroma of an HBO original drama.
- The earthy, Keruoacian punch of an ABC reality show.
- The drawing-room elegance of a CW teen soap opera.
- The Swiftian guffaw of Comedy Central's fake news.
- The Breugelian mirth of Nickelodeon toon time.
- The frank naturalism of a CBS crime drama.
- The warm-bearded sentimentality of a PBS miniseries.
- The jarring sociology of an MTV documentary.

FAVORITE QUOTES

	Most Quoted	**Least Quoted**
PRESIDENT	"The only thing we have to fear is fear itself." —*FDR*	"The urchins have more to fear of us than we do of them." —*William McKinley*
BEATLE	"Give peace a chance." —*John Lennon*	"Give me a chance to write a song, guys." —*George Harrison*
ASTRONAUT	"That's one small step for a man . . . " —*Neil Armstrong*	"They don't pay me enough rubles to feed a man . . . " —*Yuri Karimov*
POET	"Two roads diverged in a wood, and I / I took the one less traveled by." —*Robert Frost*	"I buried a man under that road. This is not a poem!" —*Robert Frost*
COMPUTER GURU	"People with passion can change the world for the better." —*Steve Jobs*	"Just give me time." —*The Zuck*

FAVORITE BOOKS

Start at the diamond shape labeled "You." Follow the directional arrows to the succeeding rectangle that best describes your personality. When you reach an oval, you will discover the most appropriate favorite book. Good luck.

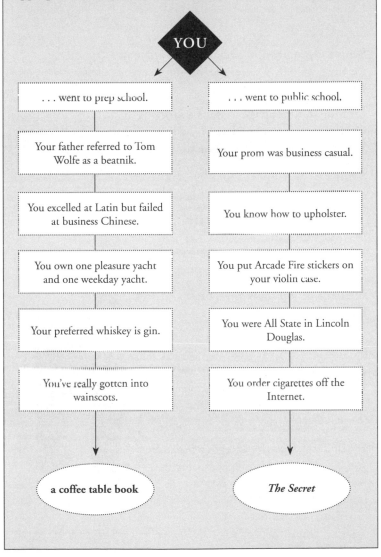

YOU

... went to prep school.

... went to public school.

Your father referred to Tom Wolfe as a beatnik.

Your prom was business casual.

You excelled at Latin but failed at business Chinese.

You know how to upholster.

You own one pleasure yacht and one weekday yacht.

You put Arcade Fire stickers on your violin case.

Your preferred whiskey is gin.

You were All State in Lincoln Douglas.

You've really gotten into wainscots.

You order cigarettes off the Internet.

a coffee table book

The Secret

ADVANCED PROFILE TECHNIQUES

What distinguishes a Facebook dilettante from a blue-faced Power User? These advanced techniques.

Inter-category dialogues

Political Views:	Very Conservative
Religious Views:	about my brand of cigarette
Email:	virginia_slim@PhilipMorris.com

Staircase progression Each field has one more item than the previous one. Creates the illusion that your life is building up to something.

Linking to a webpage under Favorite Quotes, typically a Friedman op-ed or a Wikipedia article about Confucius.

Using an explanatory anecdote

Favorite Music:	New Year's Eve 1999, Madison Square Garden. RH Chili Peppers hold the mainstage and I get passed my first community joint. The song: Love Rollercoaster. The feeling: moderate rockin'.

Listing a group more than once for emphasis.

Simpsonizing your profile pic by hand.

Epiphany asterisks.

Favorite Books:	I just ***loved*** The Kite Runner.

Bracketing an entire category because you feel that it's not really part of who you are, but it may be of anecdotal interest to your friends.

MYSPACE BOUNCER

PROFILE FAUX PAS

If you have a palindromic name like Bob or Aviva, writing it as BoB or AvIvA.

Making your address too general ("North America") or too specific ("my boyfriend's air mattress").

Listing yourself as "Very Liberal" when you're really just somewhat liberal.

Qualifying a guilty pleasure: "Grey's (but only for the medical jargon)."

Suggesting that the first item you list under "favorites" is in fact your favorite of all time by typing it in capital letters.

Formulas like "anything by X" or "mid-period Y."

Asking a clarifying question:

> Favorite Books: do you mean stranded on a desert island or stuck in a cave?

Linking to your MySpace profile (even ironically).

For self-employed creative types, listing as employer something cutesy like "my muse" or "the ages of time."

Talking back:

> Favorite Quotes: I think you mean quotation. Quote is a verb. But what do you expect? Kids these days do all of their formative reading on the Web.

Alphabetizing your favorites.

Listing *Juno* as your favorite anything.

Miscegenating authentic quotes with inside jokes:

> Favorite Quotes: "Go confidently in the direction of your dreams." —Thoreau
>
> "You didn't eat THOSE muffins, did you?" —Luke M.

✓ PHOTO ALBUM CHECKLIST

These are the photos everyone should have in an album entitled "My Life Journey."

Photos of you . . .

☐ in a tuxedo. It's a novelty tuxedo, to prove that you're not just going to a funeral or a Yo-Yo Ma concert.

☐ lounging on a couch with a friend's head on your shoulder. You're flexing your delts to provide a comfy resting spot.

☐ with four straws, four friends, and one big ice cream soda. All the straws are in your mouth.

☐ and a friend bent double, laughing. A third person's laptop is covered in salsa.

☐ standing in a meadow, staring into the distance. The distance is Baltimore.

☐ standing alone in a baseball stadium at night, swinging an imaginary bat. The scoreboard reads, "Brian wins the pennant!" (if feasible)

☐ delivering the valedictory speech at your high school in full academic garb. Your least-favorite teacher is in a straitjacket nearby, frothing.

☐ teaching a disadvantaged youth the rudiments of algebra. He's really getting it!

Chapter III

5 people you meet on facebook

Facebook attracts all kinds. Jocks, geeks, goths, type A's, cheerleaders, lunch ladies. . . .We could keep going. But let's just say Facebook is as universal and diverse as the cover of a fourth-grade civics reader. Heck, there are even a few jazz musicians.

And yet the unspoken truth is that there are only a few basic motivations that drive every Facebook profile—let's call them the Facebook personas. Five in particular stand out. With practice, you'll be able to recognize them easily. Maybe you'll even recognize yourself.

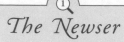

The Newser

"NO NEWS IS BAD [FOR A] NEWS[ER]." — *Ben Bradlee*

The Newser treats his profile like a 24-hour news channel devoted to his life. His motto is "Always be updating," and he adheres to it even when he has nothing to report—a stale profile rankles him profoundly. From inane status messages ("Mark is staring at his anthro textbook.") to pointless wall posts ("Happy half-birthday!"), the Newser strives to stay at the top of his friends' News Feeds. Especially since no one reads his campus dating blog anymore.

THE STATUS MESSAGE

The Newser changes his or her status message more often than any other field. Some examples:

Andrew Schulte is . . .
- hitting up the library for a Psych study sesh.
- headin' back to the 'teria for a second dinner. Love me that chicken parm!
- checking my e-mizzail.
- at the game. Go Red Wave!
- mourning the end of the weekend.
- wondering whether the opposite of "discombobulated" is "combobulated."
- checking my Facebook messages.
- laughing at this message I just got. Let me know if you want forwardzies.
- bummed about this mudslide in Indonesia.

Alexa Goldstein is . . .
- procrastinating without remorse.
- pondering the necessity of Facebook.
- wondering if Facebook won't just go the way of Geocities, Prodigy, Friendster.
- realizing Facebook is more novelty than utility.
- starting to believe the Zuck just got lucky.
- seriously thinking about hopping on the LinkedIn bandwagon.
- account removed by Team Facebook

A DAY IN THE LIFE OF A NEWSER

It's Saturday morning, er, afternoon, and you just woke up with a hangover. (Limoncello is a false friend.) All your peeps must surely be curious to know about the physiological response of your brain to an excessive intake of alcohol ("Sean is woozy from the boozy."). Like, some of them are even neurochemists. They'll want to compare notes. You take an aspirin and successively record the action and its effect ("Sean is self-medicating."

"Sean is now able to stand up."). You go out to 7-Eleven for some Vitamin Water (dragon fruit, natch) and you keep note of the outing ("Sean is on a hunt for some liquid nutrition."). Then you return ("Sean is bzzack."), drink it, feel crazy, and tell us about that, too ("Sean is feeling CrAzY."). Suddenly a little less crazy, you sit down and methodically upload, tag, and sort pics from last night's party ("Crunking in the Quad 2k7"). Finally, your status reads, "Sean is sated . . . but for how long?" Indeed, Sean, for how long?

THE ETHICS OF BEING A NEWSER

We support the presence of Newsers on the Book—but only to a point. After all, a lot could be said for not having a 24-hour news channel devoted to world news, let alone an ordinary person's life. Do CNN viewers really need to know about the butter statue of Lance Bass erected in Des Moines? If you do choose the path of the Newser, be reasonable. A broken heart, yeah, sure; a broken record on Text Twist, maybe; a dream where you broke your record on Text Twist—please god no. Don't even save it for your therapist. The world is fast suffocating under a mound of TMI. Do your part by doing nothing.

WHAT MOTIVATES NEWSERS

We asked Professor Heinrich Feldschmidt, chair of neuro-pathology at the University of Vienna, about what prompts the Newser to seek out a computer and update Facebook profiles so habitually. He tells us: "The inability to stop writing, or hypergraphia, is a well-documented phenomenon in persons who associate the act of composition with some other compulsory neurosis." And Jabberwocky did gyre and gimble in the wabe. Here are the real reasons:

- Watched too much CNN during development, and not enough C-SPAN
- Mother referred to changing his diapers as "updating"
- Compensating for lack of news about missing uncle
- Vanity

EXTREME NEWSER STORIES

"Once I updated my status on a roller coaster just before the loop. I was like, 'Emma is totally about to lose it.' And then I totally did!"

"I went on this really long road trip once and I sang '99 Bottles of Beer on the Wall' as updates to my favorite music. But with a twist: I drank a bottle of beer for each verse. By the end my favorite music was 'tqawijtw3%aa,' which makes sense, because if I were singing the song, it would start coming out in Portuguese, too."

"It got to be so I was updating activities in my sleep. Literally. This led to my now infamous 'falling through the air pursued by a giant robot naked' activity. Anyway, a lot of guys thought I was into anime after that, which was kind of unhelpful."

"So I once had a contest to see how many 'About Me' updates I could pull off in a day. Most of them were just things like 'Update 783. A new record!' But I had fun. The prize was knowing I had mastered (yet another) aspect of the Book."

TRIVIA

- On February 8, 2006, when the default setting for the "My Friends" page was changed to display only friends with recently updated profiles, the percentage of Newsers in the Facebook population increased 45 percent.
- The Top 100 Newsers make one-half of all updates to Facebook and three-quarters of all updates to Wikipedia.
- The record for most updates on a Facebook profile in a single day is held by a Newser from Ohio by the name of Sandy Peterson. She's also by far the fattest member of Facebook.
- "Being a Newser" is considered a defense to criminal child neglect in Massachusetts.

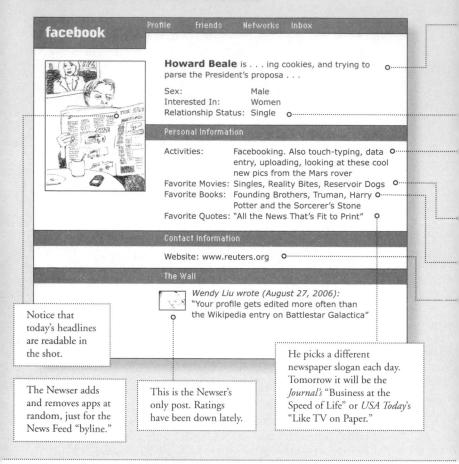

facebook

Profile   Friends   Networks   Inbox

Howard Beale is . . . ing cookies, and trying to parse the President's proposa . . .

Sex: Male
Interested In: Women
Relationship Status: Single

Personal Information

Activities: Facebooking. Also touch-typing, data entry, uploading, looking at these cool new pics from the Mars rover
Favorite Movies: Singles, Reality Bites, Reservoir Dogs
Favorite Books: Founding Brothers, Truman, Harry Potter and the Sorcerer's Stone
Favorite Quotes: "All the News That's Fit to Print"

Contact Information

Website: www.reuters.org

The Wall

Wendy Liu wrote (August 27, 2006):
"Your profile gets edited more often than the Wikipedia entry on Battlestar Galactica"

Notice that today's headlines are readable in the shot.

The Newser adds and removes apps at random, just for the News Feed "byline."

This is the Newser's only post. Ratings have been down lately.

He picks a different newspaper slogan each day. Tomorrow it will be the *Journal's* "Business at the Speed of Life" or *USA Today's* "Like TV on Paper."

FORMAL DEFINITION OF A NEWSER

1) updates her profile at least three times during the slowest "news" day—up to three hundred times during a "personal 9/11."
2) changes her profile photo like Brad Pitt changes diapers.
3) has, at least once, updated her profile during an exam ("Kelly can forget about med school.").
4) is an early investor in a company that plans to outsource profile updates to China.

The Newser uses a trick straight from the Ailes and Turner playbook: updating the status message every second, one letter at a time, to resemble a news crawl

This is one of the Newser's most frequently updated fields. Because of the eye-catching heart that appears on his friends' News Feeds, he enters and exits relationships with Valderrama speed.

Note to aspiring Newsers: If you have no personal news, check cnn.com or bbc.co.uk and think of creative ways stories might relate to you. Did you witness a hurricane? (Or a really overcast day caused by the same system?) Did you vote in an important election? Did you attend a party with someone who looked exactly like Topher Grace?

A good opportunity for token updates during a slow news hour. At this moment, he's rotating through early 90s zeitgeist flicks.

Like all good journalists, he favors history, biography, and a little bit of trash.

Facebook.com could be interpreted as ironic (a tone which should be left to more experienced journalists).

NEWSER NICKNAMES FOR FACEBOOK

- LiveJournal 2.0
- Me-kipedia
- The Ol' Cyber-Rag

FAMOUS NEWSERS FROM HISTORY

★ Moses   ★ Marcel Proust   ★ Former Senator Bob Graham

The Self-Promoter

A.K.A. THE WEEKEND WARRIOR, DJ FB,
DON KING, MADISON AVE

"THERE IS ONLY ONE THING IN THE WORLD WORSE THAN BEING [FACEBOOK STALKED], AND THAT IS NOT BEING [FACEBOOK STALKED]." — *Oscar Wilde*

The Self-Promoter thinks of her profile as a gossip column in a glossy magazine. Except for some reason this magazine is devoted solely to a Clemson sophomore's nightlife. She wants to come across as happy and fab as TMZ, *even though she's usually as unglamorous as the DMZ. The Self-Promoter is Facebook's version of the scenester. She wants to be seen at the scene, preferably by other scenesters. Keep in mind: In real life, the Self-Promoter may not be anything close to a scenester, or even a nonhermit. The escapist fantasy Facebook provides is like* Second Life, *minus* The Legend of Zelda.

A SELF-PROMOTIONAL PRANK

"A few of us got together (we work in fashion, ads, sales) to make the most awesome profile ever. It was like a social experiment. Plus, we would learn something. How many friends could we get for a guy (too easy for a girl) who didn't even exist? We made this awesome composite photo of a bunch of hot models for his profile pic and gave him pimped-out stats (Harvard, Hamptons, highbrow). Then we sent friend requests to random people . . . but Team Facebook took it down almost immediately. The give-away? We named him 'Luther van Awesomestein.'"

FRIEND OF A SELF-PROMOTER TELLS ALL

"I knew this girl who was truly effed up in the head. Her medication schedule required its own spreadsheet. And she wasn't good about keeping up with it, because that's hard for someone who's effed up in the head. But she was pretty and had this really awesome Facebook profile (parties, destinations, glam away messages). And I thought what someone who didn't really know her would think her life was like. They would just never know how sad it truly was . . . Anyway, the medication-reminder app ended up saving her life. Now she works for the pharma lobby."

THE ECONOMIST EXPLAINS

The difference between self-promotion on MySpace and self-promotion on Facebook is the difference between money and value. On MySpace, every aspiring garage band, porn star, method actor, basement improv troupe, and *soi-disant* artist hawks his wares in a 24/7 flea market where every booth is accorded the same space. On Facebook, all you have to (or can) sell is yourself.

FAMOUS SELF-PROMOTERS FROM HISTORY

★ Louis XIV   ★ Napoleon   ★ Charles de Gaulle   ★ Amélie

ANNOTATED SELF-PROMOTER PROFILE

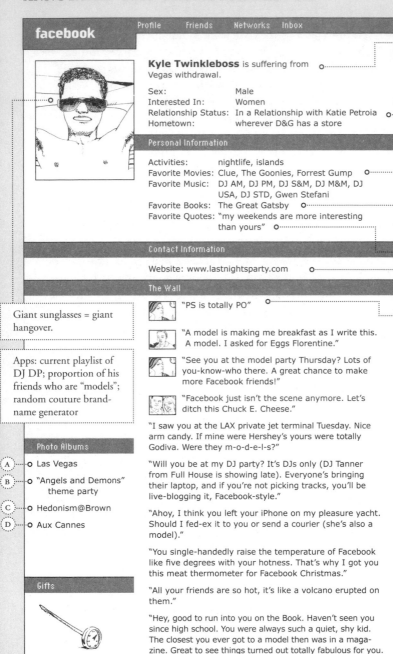

facebook

Profile   Friends   Networks   Inbox

Kyle Twinkleboss is suffering from Vegas withdrawal.

Sex: Male
Interested In: Women
Relationship Status: In a Relationship with Katie Petroia
Hometown: wherever D&G has a store

Personal Information

Activities: nightlife, islands
Favorite Movies: Clue, The Goonies, Forrest Gump
Favorite Music: DJ AM, DJ PM, DJ S&M, DJ M&M, DJ
                 USA, DJ STD, Gwen Stefani
Favorite Books: The Great Gatsby
Favorite Quotes: "my weekends are more interesting
                 than yours"

Contact Information

Website: www.lastnightsparty.com

The Wall

"PS is totally PO"

"A model is making me breakfast as I write this. A model. I asked for Eggs Florentine."

"See you at the model party Thursday? Lots of you-know-who there. A great chance to make more Facebook friends!"

"Facebook just isn't the scene anymore. Let's ditch this Chuck E. Cheese."

"I saw you at the LAX private jet terminal Tuesday. Nice arm candy. If mine were Hershey's yours were totally Godiva. Were they m-o-d-e-l-s?"

"Will you be at my DJ party? It's DJs only (DJ Tanner from Full House is showing late). Everyone's bringing their laptop, and if you're not picking tracks, you'll be live-blogging it, Facebook-style."

"Ahoy, I think you left your iPhone on my pleasure yacht. Should I fed-ex it to you or send a courier (she's also a model)."

"You single-handedly raise the temperature of Facebook like five degrees with your hotness. That's why I got you this meat thermometer for Facebook Christmas."

"All your friends are so hot, it's like a volcano erupted on them."

"Hey, good to run into you on the Book. Haven't seen you since high school. You were always such a quiet, shy kid. The closest you ever got to a model then was in a magazine. Great to see things turned out totally fabulous for you. Do you still use Photoshop a lot? I remember when you said you could edit anyone into any photo. That must be really useful. It's so cool you were at Justin Timberlake's house!"

Photo Albums

(A) Las Vegas
(B) "Angels and Demons" theme party
(C) Hedonism@Brown
(D) Aux Cannes

Gifts

Giant sunglasses = giant hangover.

Apps: current playlist of DJ DP; proportion of his friends who are "models"; random couture brand-name generator

Five minutes ago, his status was "suffering from a Vegas overdose." Five minutes from now it will be "entering a Vegas rehabilitation center."

This person is never a bona fide significant other. He or she serves the same function as a fourth-degree mage in a *World of Warcraft* hunting posse: virtual companionship.

Fluffiest of popcorn movies: The Self-Promoter wants to be relatable to the masses, despite his weekend jaunts to Majorca (cf. a presidential candidate alluding to his log-cabin taste for Big Macs).

Classic American tale of a Self-Promoter

Presumptuous.

He knew an intern at the site who promised to get his pic on it for $500.

"Palm Springs is totally Played Out."

Ⓐ The "more sinned against than sinning, but a lot of both" trip.

Ⓑ "We're going for Bosch, but we'll settle for Posh."

Ⓓ "Not there for the film festival, just toolin'."

Ⓒ A celebrated annual gathering and quasi-reunion for the free-love set. There's a bubble machine and body painting just like at a county fair.

The Friend Whore

"A FRIEND TO ALL IS A FRIEND TO NONE" — *English proverb*

We've all seen profiles with four-figure friend counts and thought "Who is this person? An aspiring politician? A fake-ID-maker? One of James Brown's illegitimate sons?" But if you feel dwarfed by mammoth friend lists, take comfort—you're likely looking at a Friend Whore. The Friend Whore pathologically confuses Facebook with World of Warcraft, *and the acquisition of friends with the mining of gold. This is an unfortunate error. It's not just that the value of each of the Friend Whore's friends is diluted by his or her purported largesse. Facebook friendship itself is at stake here.*

DO FRIEND WHORES EVER REJECT FRIENDS?

This is like the old theologian's saw about whether the devil might not ever perform a good deed. Perhaps, but it mitigates nothing.

CONFESSIONS OF A FORMER FRIEND WHORE

I started with my friends, my real friends, like everyone else. Then my colleagues, my buds, my teachers, my neighbors, and my lovers. From there, I solicited acquaintances, contemporaries, peers, one-timers, passersby . . . but I was insatiable. I moved on to people with the same last name, then people with a similar last name. Friends of my little brother and enemies of my big sister. A guy I saw litter, and the other guy who picked it up. Woody Allen fans and Vince Vaughn detractors. This girl whose profile just clicked with me, even though it was in German. A professor whose class I dropped. Mark Zuckerberg (rejected) and Rivers Cuomo (accepted, then deleted). I even friended fauxfiles*, endless fauxfiles—you know, the shoddy ones where the profile pic was just the first hit on Google image search. Reader, I even feigned affiliation with Ron Paul and friended everyone in his official campaign group. (They all accepted.) But rock bottom was a girl named Terry Winters, birth place Mars. That's right—I friended an inmate of the Shady Grove Home for the Insane, just for the juice. Monster is too nice a word.

*Fauxfile (n): A fake profile for a celebrity or notable person, often played straight.

NOT TO BE CONFUSED WITH . . .

Network Whores, who may have a reasonable number of friends but seek to have them at farther-flung networks than yours. Look for the guy with friends at Southern Texas Bible College, Yeshiva University, Hamas (political wing), and Reykjavik.

Also, group whores, message sluts, wall tarts, gift prostitutes, app fanboys, and graffiti pervs.

MOST PATHETIC WAYS TO TROLL FOR FRIENDS

- Pretend to be a freshman and attend frosh events
- Become an RA
- Press the flesh in the dining hall
- Sandwich-board in the quad
- Run for student office
- Facebook Gift bribes
- Become an actual whore

COOLEST WAYS TO TROLL FOR FRIENDS

- Become really popular through legitimate means and have a lot of genuine friends
- Deal drugs

TOP FIVE FRIEND-WHORE MAJORS

1) Psychology
2) Behavioral Psychology
3) Sociology
4) Psycho-Sociology
5) Math

DEFENSIVE ABOUT ME'S

Since potential johns are bound to be suspicious of high Friend counts, the Friend Whore will occasionally use the About Me field to explain his or her wide-cast Friend net:

My dad told me that a man who has friends can never be poor. He also said a man who plays the banjo will never want company, so I guess he wasn't all that wise.

Yeah, I've got a lot of friends. So what? The concept of a Facebook friend is meaningless anyway. It's just an entry on a database at a server farm in Palo Alto. How is that a real friendship? Now, Carrie, Samantha, and the gang—they have a real friendship.

At summer camp, I was that kid with the most friendship bracelets and the fewest enemy anklets.

In India, it is not uncommon to be friends with everyone in your village. So while I might befriend an untouchable, I would never poke one.

DERREK ROGERS

I actually do have this many friends. I'll prove it to you. Ask me about any of them. What do you want to know? Derrek Rogers?—He's into Boondock Saints, fantasy football, and drinks beer from red plastic cups. Do you think I could make this up?

I didn't have many friends as a kid, on account of the coal-mining job and my shyness. I fantasized about one day having hundreds of friends that I could store in a box and play with anytime I wanted. Luckily, soon after I figured out this was what "serial killing" was, I discovered Facebook. Now I keep all my friends in a virtual box and stalk them anytime I want.

ANNOTATED FRIEND WHORE PROFILE

facebook

Profile   Friends   Networks   Inbox

Kelly D'Amico is painting the town friend.

Looking For: Friendship

Personal Information

Favorite Movies: My Best Friend's Wedding, The
                    Three Amigos, Care Bears and
                    Friends, Your Friends and Neighbors,
                    group pornography

Favorite TV Shows: Friends (before it got all preachy)

Work Info

Employer: Ohio State University
Title: personal liaison

Employer: Ohio State University
Title: glad-handler

Employer: Ohio State University
Title: meeter-and-greeter

Employer: Geek Squad
Title: networker

Friends: {2,113 in
college network}

Groups

Overwhelmed by Obama, Crazy for Clinton, Bonkers for
Bloomberg, Revved Up for Rudy, Interested in Edwards

She's in a group
of (guess what?)
friends

Original Friend Whore Apps

Friend search powered by Google

Friend visualizations (how close could you get to the moon if you
lined up all your friends from head to toe?)

"The Bordello": 3-D bordello with representations of all your friends;
plays MIDI honky-tonk piano music in the background

Motor-mouth maven John Moschitta Jr. reads off the names of your
friends at warp speed (via the magic of computers). It still takes a
while!

Birthday Pal (generates a personalized birthday message or wall post
for each of your friends; its tastefulness can be calibrated in advance)

TRIVIA

The title of Whoriest Friend Whore was briefly held by a scam artist from New Jersey. He claimed to be a teenager suffering from an incurable disease whose dying wish was to break the record for most friends on Facebook.

ASK THE MORALIST

Q. *Is it okay to cancel my friendship with someone because I suspect she's become a friend whore?*

A. Yes.

Q. *That's what I thought.*

THE FACEBOOK FUTURIST SEZ

In a more utopian version of the site, Team Facebook will do something about Friend Whores, either by instituting a maximum friend count or requiring an occasional quiz that asks the user to distinguish (from a random sampling) who is and who is not one's friend. A failing grade leads to a tithing of one's harem. Otherwise, friendship is but a blog with no readers.

FAMOUS FRIEND WHORES FROM HISTORY

★ Cleopatra   ★ FDR   ★ Wilt Chamberlain

4

The Creepster

"AND HIS EYES HAVE ALL THE SEEMING / OF A [CREEPSTER'S]
THAT IS DREAMING." — *Edgar Allan Poe*

*Hey, wait a second—didn't you say the major difference between
Facebook and MySpace is the lack of these guys? How can he be
one of the archetypes? For one thing, we're anticipating ourselves
slightly with this listing. The Creepster will really come into
his own with the maturing of the twenty-something Facebook
population. But as the Book penetrates the exurbs, he's become a
looming menace. Take a deep breath and don't let feelings of icki-
ness compel you to turn the page. There is something educational
here. Particularly if you're an older, male member of the Book.*

SUGGESTION BOX

The Internet is a sketchy place.

Does this even bear mention in 2008?

Yes. It bears repetition.

The Internet is a really sketchy place.

Internet success stories, such as they are, all have something in common: They make the Internet a less sketchy place ("blue" websites notwithstanding). Facebook provides a clean, well-lighted place for you and your friends to hang out in. It's that college-town bar with the books on gentlemen's games and *The Gentleman's Guide to Books on Gaming*. If the Creepster moves in for good, then, as when Hipsters invade a neighborhood, the natives will move out.

The Creepster's daily grind is the unsolicited message to a stranger. We, the authors, believe Facebook would be a stronger, safer, less shady place without the ability to send messages to nonfriends. And while we're at it, how about a limit on snarky status messages, too?

WINNING CREEPSTER PROFESSIONS

Does the creepster ever succeed at his game? Don't make the faulty argument that if it didn't ever work, he wouldn't keep trying. The same could be said about lottery players and actors without agents. With the right profession, a Creepster can inch his success rate up into the merely astronomical.

Popular professor. This is a benign and self-explanatory reason for having young friends. It works against you if your field is something creepy, like criminal psychology or Esperanto.

DJ. You'll need a shaved head and a wiry physique, but DJs still seem like a profession from the twenty-second century to most people. It also won't hurt if your nipples are transparent.

Celebrated novelist. This will lead to the assumption that you are: a) nonthreatening and b) an intimate of Jonathan Franzen. As Jonathan Franzen has almost no intimates, people will deduce that you are, in fact, Jonathan Franzen.

ANATOMY OF THE CREEPSTER PHOTO

He's trying to seem cool without trying to seem cool, but he erroneously thinks that as an older guy the best way to do this is to look like he's trying to be cool, and thus come off endearing for his earnestness. Sunglasses, windbreaker, stubble, beach setting. A regular outdoorsman. He's picked a setting as far from that dank, dark basement room as he could find. But don't be fooled: It's probably a green screen.

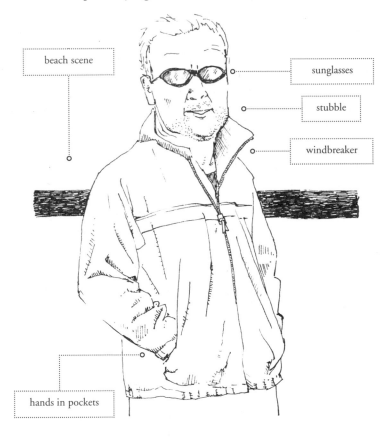

beach scene

sunglasses

stubble

windbreaker

hands in pockets

OPEN LETTER TO CREEPSTERS

Umm, hi. Coach, neighbor, clergyman, dad. Your guises are as varied as Dana Carvey's in a malformed star vehicle. Your motives are dark and dank; they are that room in the basement you're still afraid might contain ghosts. If you are reading this book, it's not because you enjoy satire or a wry look at the zeitgeist. We're onto you, ponytail.

COMMON CREEPSTER PICK-UP LINES

I was just browsing my daughter's friends and noticed you're also interested in procrastinating.

So what's this I hear about poking?

I'm writing this book about Facebook . . .

Do you think old people can be cool too?

I just got a message that I was poked by you. So here is my message poking you back. Poke.

Do you think I'm old?

Mark Zuckerberg is my nephew.

Yeah, I would be totally creeped out too if an older guy messaged me out of the blue. But here's the thing . . .

Have you heard of Hanna Montana? I'm only asking because my company gave me box seats to her concert and I'm wondering if you know anyone who would be would be interested in going to see it with the president of MTV North America.

A CREEPSTER SPEAKS OUT

I really just wanted to have some young friends. You know, find out what the kids are listening to, learn the "phat" "lingo," throw back some e-beers. My parents didn't understand me, and I wanted to break the cycle, to bridge the generation gap once and for all. Does that make me Sketch-erey Dahmer? If it does, then serial killers are all right in my book. My Facebook.

IS HE A CREEPSTER OR A TOURIST?

Not that tourists are all that great either, but mostly they just want to gawk a little after reading Slate's article about the Book and then move on to Qweeber or Zlopt or whatever else the guys behind Web 2.0 have cooked up lately. For your own curiosity, how to tell the difference:

Creepsters	Tourists
Moe Szyslak	Ned Flanders
hang out in alleys	look for hidden gelato places in alleys
used America Online in 1994	used Prodigy in 1994
are reading this book in a dark basement	are reading this book in a well-lit wine cellar

FAMOUS CREEPSTERS FROM HISTORY

★ Socrates   ★ Aaron Burr   ★ Ted Bundy

ANNOTATED CREEPSTER PROFILE

Obviously a computer-cam pic.

The zeal of the convert.

Wants to leave his options open.

facebook

Profile   Friends   Networks   Inbox

Humbert Holmes is hooked on the book.

Personal Information

Sex: male
Interests: friendship, activity partners,
                  hello kitty
Hometown: the east coast
Activities: music, dance, reading, yoga, hiking
Favorite Music: kanye west, carrie underwood,
                  various artists

Contact Information

The Wall

The Creepster is, not for nothing, also known as the Chameleonster. Unsure of what makes for a reasonable favorite anything among today's youth, he's assembled his entries from a variety of popular-looking people. Note that his tastes are too average, like all of his favorite foods are appetizers.

The top iTunes tracks from the week he joined. The last one refers to *High School Musical 2*.

Empty as his sense of decency.

5

The Performance Artist

"ART IS COMING FACE TO FACE[BOOK] WITH YOURSELF." — *Jackson Pollock*

The Performance Artist is an artist of herself—at least when it comes to her Facebook profile. Most Booksters these days join for the pokes and marriage proposals, the wall posts and the stalking. But the Artist seeks something a little different—something deeper and more permanent. Something artsy. She compiles her profile with all the precision of Michelangelo playing Jenga on the edge of a volcano. Every word, tagged picture, gift, and app is meticulously selected to render her profile a work of art—a beautiful and subtle challenge to your soul. Are you up for it?

WHAT ABOUT FRIENDS?

The Performance Artist usually picks her friends for their sense of photographic composition, ignoring real-life lovers and peers. Sometimes she'll add a few because their last names just work. A celebrated Artist once exclusively befriended people named Jennifer Lee.

WHAT'S UNSAID IS AS IMPORTANT AS WHAT IS

Performance Artists have been known to leave their entire profiles blank and post only apps. All leave out the date of birth (an Artist just is) or enter something absurd to make a point (1/1/2000 = "I'm a child of the millennium").

A LETTER TO MARK ZUCKERBERG

To my Patron and Muse,

I am writing with a tormented soul to insist on, nay, demand greater creative control over my Facebook canvas. As I was taking my absinthe late this morning, some vagrant of unknown network (Bowdoin?) wrote on my wall. I immediately deleted it, but the slight was recorded on the News Feeds of all of my fellow Artists, which I have no choice but to now regard as an indelible part of my oeuvre.

Furthermore, when my public views my art, your infernal machinery selects six friends at random to appear under "Friends" with brazen callousness to the controlled unity of my composition. I only have six friends, but I am incensed that I cannot rearrange them in order of increasing facial hair.

I will not work much longer under these conditions.

Signed,

Pratt

Pratt

EXHIBITION SPACES

Performance Artists will update their profiles in public in order to get their art out there. Common venues include:

- The Apple Store
- Old folks' home computer lab
- Wicker Park
- An IHOP
- Europe

THINGS A PERFORMANCE ARTIST OBSERVES ABOUT FACEBOOK THAT A LAYMAN DOESN'T

- Facebook blue is the same shade as the sky in the Sistine Chapel.
- The Facebook font has no symbol for the euro.
- The resolution of most profile pics is actually kind of poor.
- The Facebook aesthetic is "late-90s Google."
- Graffiti is a valid urban art form.

THE PERFORMANCE ARTIST'S DEVELOPMENT

Like any great master, the Performance Artist is constantly reinventing himself. In a burst of artistic energy, he will expunge his wall, rewrite every word of his profile, and apply the "sepia" filter to his photo (which was already pretty sepia-toned). Here are the common stages of his career:

Discovery: "Facebook is itself a giant wall every human can add art to. But what brushstroke is best? Answer: the friendliest one."

Experimental: "What if I have no friends? Is that a commentary? And should I be honest in my favorites, or dishonest but cool?"

Maturation: "My profile pic shouldn't be beautiful; it should raise important questions. Like a giant blue question mark."

Disgust: "If I receive one more wall post from one of my so-called artist friends saying 'we should hang out some time,' I'm going to shut down my profile. Would you take an iPod into the Louvre???"

Acceptance: "I just got the cutest gift today: a pig painting in a smock. Could I design these for a living?"

PERFORMANCE ARTIST-Y PHOTOS

- Dead flowers
- A fork
- The back of a head
- The Facebook question mark, but upside down
- Two left hands
- Shirtless in a graveyard
- A mirror
- A Rorschach blot
- A colorful dish she ate in Prague
- Face superimposed on a dog's face

MESSAGING WITH A PERFORMANCE ARTIST

Samples from the inbox of Lily Bart (Hobart), a.k.a. the Facebook Georgia O'Keeffe:

Dan Koontz (Hobart): hey. i noticed ur favorite music was hammering and silence. thats so weird . . . what does it all mean? u r pretty deep. lets meet up sometime
Lily Bart (Hobart): No time is some time.

Sarah Gordon (New York, NY): happy birthday, girl!!
Lily Bart (Hobart): Don't you mean "happy" "birth" "day" "girl"?

Rod Weiner (Chicago State): Your profile is pretentious and obvious. You're trying to come across as artsy-cool, making obscure references to random French pseudorealists, but anyone with access to Wikipedia could do that. Just be yourself. The really cool people on Facebook are honest. You should have the courage to show the world who you really are.
Lily Bart (Hobart): I am rubber and you are glue.

ANNOTATED PERFORMANCE ARTIST PROFILE

facebook

Profile · Friends · Networks · Inbox

Lisa A. Hardy is writing her status message.

Personal Information

Activities:	being, doing, feeling, knowing, sighing
Favorite Movies:	the movies I enjoy the most
Favorite TV Shows:	my favorite movies on television
Favorite Books:	the source code of Facebook

Contact Information

Website: www.facebook.com/profile.php?id=1316062 ○

The Wall

 Wendy Liu wrote (August 31, 2006):
"This wall post has six words."

A vintage Performance Artist profile. This kind of thing was all the rage in the early days of the Book, when members tried to keep an ironic detachment about them. The theme here appears to be "self-reference," but it might also be "Facebook," in that the site leads to a lot of navel-gazing.

Not her own profile page (too obvious), but that of an MC Escher fauxfile, whose own favorite website links back here.

6

Minor Archetypes

A.K.A. THE REST

THE ACTIVIST

Some profiles defy neat categorization. The following is by no means an exhaustive list but includes the more common curiosities, hybrids, and bizarros.

The Time Capsule: Hasn't updated her profile since January 2005. Still has a picture from winter break in Ecuador, her junior spring class schedule, and a reference to something called "Good Charlotte."

The Riddler: Profile completely empty. Wants you to think he's up to something really important. So named for his question-mark avatar, which to anyone else would be a Mark of Cain, but to him is a Badge of Mystery.

The Friend Snob: He chooses his friends with the care with which a fashion editor chooses interns. His acceptance rate hovers around 5 percent, slightly lower during the holidays.

The Resume: He uses the Book as a less on-the-nose Monster.com. Potential employers should be impressed by his quotations from managerial textbooks ("The oxygen of business is people; the nitrogen is paper").

The Latinist: Her profile is written like an anthology of prep-school mottos. But her ample use of Latin actually just masks her ignorance of Greek.

The Activist: When she first heard about the Book, she had visions of a wondrous future. Why, it shall provide the fertile soil for a grassroots campaign that will grow over the entire

earth, she thought to herself. She has started a petition to allow voting in federal elections via the iCandidate app.

Joe Average: The median Facebook user. Likes Coldplay, the Beatles, both Rhythm and Blues and R&B. Blonde but also sort of brunette, tall but also sort of short. Could have been assembled by a bot.

JOE AVERAGE

The IPO Wannabe: Under the curious impression that Team Facebook looks at his profile, he tries to come off as the site's Number One Fan. He fills out every field, joins all the right groups, and beta tests major new apps. Also, namedrops the Zuck and player-hates the social network upstart du jour. In the best possible scenario, this leads to a tour of Camp Facebook and some swag.

The Groupie: She's never met a group she didn't want to admin. She also went to a lot of Phish shows circa 2000.

The Exile: Translates his MySpace or Friendster page directly to Facebook. Is 100 years old, uses his status message to record moods (complete with emoticons), and writes "lol" a lot. Très déclassé.

The Narc: A parent, teacher, or RA who uses the Book to snoop on young revelers. Like the Mormons in Times Square, she's hoping to save some souls in the midst of temptation. Giveaways: excrement-eating-grin profile pic, an empty wall, and links to cautionary tales about online predators.

THE NARC

The Secret Agent: A fauxfile that allows a covert Bookster to stalk without being stalked. Has an obviously fake name ("Hugh Jazz"), no picture, and his interests are "none of your business." Often just wants to prowl around the Book, but if he tries to join your anti-Bush group, it's probably some PATRIOT Act thing.

The Originalist: A fan of Facebook 1.0—before apps, groups, and even frenemies. Has an Amish-ish aversion to any feature created after 2005. Can't remember when pokes were added, so uses them sparingly.

The Pack Rat: Finds it impossible to delete anything from her profile, even that unfortunate photo she accidentally posted of herself "testing" her webcam without a shirt on. Profile is meandering and self-contradictory, and bears witness to her maturation from death metal to indie death metal.

The Recidivist: Serially leaves Facebook in a huff, but can never stay out of the game for long. That's why you've gotten five friend requests from him. Reminds you of that guy who's always quitting cigarettes only to take them up again during finals.

dating
&
relationships

In the old days, when you got your freshman facebook by U.S. post, you circled the hotties, x'd out the shoddies, and put a question mark over the robotties. Now you've got 60 million people to mark and infinite Sharpies.

Facebook Is Not a Dating Site

NOR A SPEED DATING SITE, FOR THAT MATTER.

MISLEADING PROFILE PHOTO: THEY APPEAR TO BE DATING BUT ARE NOT

Let's get this straight. Match.com, eHarmony, iLove, and ultra-orthodox JDate—those are dating sites. Amazon, Google, eBay, Facebook—those are not dating sites. Dating sites are where you seek out romantic entanglements with strangers, and occasionally discover the ages of fossils. Nondating sites are where you do everything else.

But you know so many people who owe flirtations, hookups, affairs, and even marriages to the Book. How can that be? Let's put it this way: The best singles bar in town is usually the laundromat. Especially if you're looking for dates with the kind of people who don't go to singles bars but do wash their sheets.

HOW TO FIND A FACE ON FACEBOOK

So you met a hottie at a pahty and you wanna get naughty? Well, Jazzy Jeff, it would have been helpful if you'd gotten her number, or her name, or a at least a vague idea of what state she lives in. Nevertheless, you could still pick her out of a lineup. If only there were some kind of book with everyone's face in it . . .

Search the friends of the party's host. This won't help if the host is a Friend Whore or a charitable foundation.

Interests search. It's the only time anyone uses "advanced search" outside of grad school. Try to remember something unique about her interests. She definitely enjoyed Smirnoff Ice, but dig deeper. Didn't she say something about scrimshaw . . . or was it George Bernard Shaw?

The photo-tag switch-'em-about. Find her in a pic from the party and tag her with the name of a friend who looks vaguely similar. Your friend will call you on your gaffe and protest that she looks nothing like that Caitlyn.

Facial recognition app. An MIT sophomore is presumably coding this right now. Look for it on Google. It will be called something like "Face Genie" or "enVisage" or "Stalkerbot Prime."

READING BETWEEN THE FIELDS

You just got a friend request from a stranger. The poke/message one-two punch follows fast. But you have your suspicions about this guy. It's nothing blatant—he doesn't have the Osama bin Laden fauxfile in his Top Friends or list "imprisonment"

as an interest. But a profile is like a James Joyce novel or a mid-90s Disney movie: It's easy to miss the filthy subtext.

No employment info listed: This guy actually does have a job; the unemployed call themselves "freelancers." But it's either high-level CIA stuff or something embarrassing, like LSAT tutor. Keep in mind that certain august surnames (Gates, Moneybags) may signal inherited wealth.

No tagged photos: Only two types of people don't show up in photos: vampires and losers.

Profile photo with his arm around a girl: Protesting too much; defensive. At any county fair, you can buy this kind of pic for the price of a candy apple.

Profile photo with a girl biting his ear: Whoa. This guy is a MegaStud. A regular *Die Hard*-era Bruce Willis. The only other possible explanation for why a girl bit his ear (on camera!) is that it was made out of toffee.

No date of birth: Maybe he was raised in a strict Jainist household that practiced stern self-abnegation and refused to celebrate or even record birthdays. Or maybe he's really old.

SKEEZIEST FACEBOOK PICK-UP LINES EVER

Wow, you've got like the hottest profile pic I've seen on the Book. Real or Photoshop? And if the latter, can I hire you to paint my loft?

Got poked?

You remind me of this character from an anime I watched. She had big eyes and an innocent look just like you. Want to act out a scene? You be the girl and I'll be Octopus-san.

I know you must get like five of these messages a day, but I think you'll find this one a little different. I'm a time traveler from the future and you need to go out with me this weekend to save the world. It's a butterfly effect thing. I know that last part is kind of hard to believe, but there's literally no time to explain.

My therapist said I should try to make a new friend every day. But I really want to impress him, so let's be more than friends.

According to Google Maps, there's a large, empty parking lot a few blocks north of where you live. Meet me there at midnight and bring a board game.

We must be soul mates. All of our favorite movies and books are exactly the same. And you look just like me. Oh, wait.

Hey Courtney, remember me from tennis camp all those years ago? I assume that you're the same Courtney because you list squash as one of your interests, and that's a racquet sport too.

Gifting a stranger the champagne, thong, and pink rabbit.

You know what would look good in that pic? Me. (see attached collage)

Lots of guys have "chest bumped" him: He receives even more chest bumps in real life. Prepare to get sandwiched.

Lots of notes bemoaning the officiating at Little League games: A good sign. Has a sense of justice and fairness. Go for it. Hard.

PIMP YOUR PROFILE

On the Book, you've got to sell yourself. Use the same tricks as the big ad agencies and rappers:

Subliminal erotic images. In your profile pic, wear a shirt that reads p*n*s, or one with the boobs cut out and the phrase "These are not boobs" written underneath it.

Better by comparison. Standing next to someone fatter makes you look thinner, but it will also make it seem like you have corpulent friends. Solution: Stand next to a fat animal or in front of a large buffet. Similarly, if you want to appear taller or more muscular, pose next to a baby.

Location, location, location. You can't control where you live, but you can control how it sounds. Meager "Farmhouse Loft, Utica" becomes snappy "New York Penthouse, 10,000 sq. ft." If you live in a dorm, call it a "suite"; if you live in a garage, call it in an "annex"; if you live in a mansion, call it a "cribs."

Brand yourself. You want to be the "something" guy. It could be simple (cats, baseball) or exotic (tigers, jai alai). It doesn't even have to be a real interest. You just need something that will stick in people's minds, like the word *cornucopia.*

Themes and motifs. For example, all of your interests start with the same letter (women, wining, wassailing); everything you like is urban-themed (hip-hop, *Sim City*, antique traffic lights); all are three-letters long (ale, PSP, Mr. T).

Blurbs. Get a lot of wall posts, ideally written by an assortment of possessive lovers, fawning fratmates, and a starry-eyed younger sibling (to show your decent side). Short of creating a

BETTER BY COMPARISON

✓ CHECKLIST: PURGE YOUR PROFILE

A disco ball on the ceiling of your SUV limo may help land that first date. But after that, make gas mileage your priority. In other words, purge:

☐ a profile pic of you with a member of the opposite sex. Even if it's a celebrity or your dad. Especially if it's your celebrity dad.

☐ a favorite movie that is patently pornographic. This includes the complete works of M. Night Shyama-thong and Martin Scorsexy.

☐ chick lit (for girls) or X-Men-universe fan fiction (for guys). *Harry Potter and the Goblet of Fire* should be counterbalanced by something pretentious and literary, like *Harry Potter and the Order of the Phoenix.*

☐ wall posts from a psychotic ex. It is kind of neat to have someone that infatuated with you. On the other hand, as a sage rapper once quipped, "the more baggage you got, the more baggage she's gonna want."

☐ membership in a group that is racist, nativist, ultraconservative, hyperradical, skeptical of global warming or the existence of subatomic particles, opposed to acceptable farming practices, supportive of a return to the gold standard, creatively anachronistic, antithetical to Web 2.0, or ironic about the Book. Common sense.

☐ naughty gifts. If they aren't available now, they will be soon. Besides, the "massage tube" and the "donut that you don't eat" have no place on a family website.

☐ a goofy name. This only applies to one person we've ever encountered on Facebook. Still worth noting. Sorry to break the news, Mario P. Nintendo (Swarthmore '09).

bunch of fauxfiles and masturbatorily posting to your own wall, this is difficult to pull off. Our best advice is to make reciprocal arrangements or outsource.

Intrigue/enigma/mystery. Raw curiosity can be enough to maintain interest in your profile. Include a lateral thinking puzzle or two under About Me. For example: "A man is sitting on a porch and a phone rings. He is dead. What color are his shoes?" or "A 23-year-old founds a multibillion-dollar Internet start-up. He is alive and lives in the Bay Area. What size boxers does he wear?"

Freebies. The twenty-third wall-poster gets a free Facebook gift (the unicorn).

M. NIGHT SHYAMA-THONG

Ad-copy words. Pepper your profile with jargon from winning commercials: "zesty," "smoky," "zinger," "pepper," "starbucks," "xxx."

Composition. Advertisers control not only what the audience sees but how they see it. Lead the viewer's eyes through your page in a clockwise fashion . . . with arrows.

Catchy visuals. Don't be afraid to pander with a bit of ASCII art. Yes, it's very Web 1.0, but it retains an unmistakable outré charm. A few that will never go out of style include a lightsaber, a typewriter, and Marilyn Monroe on the vent. If desperate, you may post a tasteful PBV (penis boobs vagina).

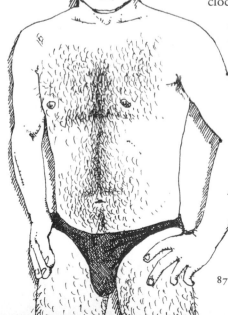

Relationship status doesn't leave much wiggle room. Like PC or Mac, red pill or blue pill, Kanye or Fiddy, it's one or the other. But many Booksters refuse to list a status at all. What does this mean?

LOVE ONLINE VS. LOVE OFFLINE

	In the Real World	**On Facebook**
SINGLE	The status we all know best—equal parts cherished and despised. The one where you get really into Kierkegaard and dress up to go to Borders.	You are available to seduce anyone with the story of that time you sat across from Pierce Brosnan on a plane.
IN A RELATIONSHIP	Pillow fights on Sunday mornings, tandem bikes, and tickle wars.	Webcam strip poker, *Second Life* philandering, and tickle viruses.
IN AN OPEN RELATIONSHIP	A slightly more acceptable variety of nudism. You probably live, or spend a lot of time, in Oregon.	You've convinced someone to dote over you while you betray him or her constantly over the Mini Feed.
IT'S COMPLICATED	Somehow you always find yourselves in each other's dorm rooms, apartments, or cabanas. How did you get there? Only a scientist could say for sure.	All greatness is necessarily complicated. A declaration that your relationship is chess to your friends' Connect Four.
ENGAGED	Ah, the scent of possibility. Like a flower just before it blooms, or a fresh Jane Austen novel before you actually read it.	Not much different than Halloween In the Oxford network—everyone can look forward to a photo album of you dressed like it's the eighteenth century.
MARRIED	Instead of someone you don't talk to at cool parties, you have someone you don't talk to at uncool parties.	A way of making the BFF thing official. Like a super friendship bracelet that glows in the dark and stains your wrist.

GOING UNLISTED

If you are a girl, it means you're not in a relationship but also
not desperate. Declaring yourself single outright is like wearing
a Princess Leia hairpiece to Comic-Con.

If you are a guy, it means you may be in a relationship or married but you're still looking for sex with anonymous partners. In
other words, it means the same thing as all the statuses.

WHEN TO LIST A RELATIONSHIP

Facebook simplifies relationships. Where once matching tattoos
or a nostril-to-nostril lovechain were the only ways to broadcast
your couplehood, now a couple of mouse clicks suffice. There
are, however, a few rules of the road.

1) Never be in a Facebook relationship with someone you
   haven't met in the real world. By extension, don't start a
   relationship with a nonperson, like your favorite bubble
   tea purveyor.

2) There's no excuse for listing yourself as "In a Relationship"
   without your partner's name. If you're that embarrassed by
   him or her, consider taking the relationship to Friendster.

3) Typically, the man should
   invite the woman into
   the relationship. When in
   doubt, the burden is on the
   partner who enjoys Zach
   Braff a little less.

4) Feel free to be married to a
   friend of the same gender, as

THE ZUCK

90

STICKY SITUATIONS: How to classify your relationship status in some classically thorny scenarios:

YOU	BUT YOU NEVER GOT HIS NAME AND CAN'T ASK NOW	WERE ASSIGNED TO KILL HIM	USED TO DATE HIS DAD	FOUND OUT HE'S DONE A LOT OF PORN	ARE A PRINCESS AND HE'S JUST A SOCIETY PHOTOGRAPHER	MUST MARRY AN ELECTRICAL ENGINEER IN HYDERABAD	TURN INTO A WEREWOLF IN THREE DAYS
HOOKED UP ONCE	Single	Single	Single	No listing	It's complicated	It's complicated	In an open relationship
HOOKED UP TWICE	Single	No listing	No listing	It's complicated	It's complicated	In an open relationship	In an open relationship
ARE HOOKING UP RIGHT NOW	No listing	It's complicated	It's complicated	In an open relationship	In an open relationship	In an open relationship	In a relationship
ARE PREGNANT AND IT'S MOST LIKELY HIS	It's complicated	In an open relationship	In an open relationship	In an open relationship	In a relationship	In a relationship	In a relationship
THINK YOU'RE IN LOVE LIKE HEIDI AND SPENCER (SEASON 2)	In an open relationship	In an open relationship	In a relationship	In a relationship	In a relationship	In a relationship	In a relationship
THINK YOU'RE IN LOVE LIKE HEIDI AND SPENCER (SEASON 3)	Single	Single	Single	Single	Single	Single	Single
ACCIDENTALLY ELOPED DURING CHURCH TEQUILA NIGHT	In an open relationship	In a relationship	In a relationship	In a relationship	In a relationship	Married	Married

KEY

- In a relationship
- Single
- In an open relationship
- It's complicated
- Married
- — No listing

long as it doesn't last more than two weeks and neither of you lives in Massachusetts.

5) If you're actually married, your spouse had better be on the Book, too. Statistically, asymmetrical Facebook marriages end quicker than those started with a Craig's List casual encounter.

BREAKING UP ON FACEBOOK

Would that breaking up on Facebook were as easy as changing your relationship status back to single.

It's a trivial matter to get drunk. Sobering up requires effort. While a romance can bloom with a simple wall haiku, the breakup can be as messy as a burst beer ball in a freshman common room. The problem is, Facebook is all about making connections. Since Mark Zuckerberg has never broken up with anyone, he's not sympathetic.

"Tear down this wall": Your first temptation will be to delete your ex's wall posts. But if you keep them around, they'll add complications to his or her personal life. It's the relationship equivalent of leaving in the forceps after surgery.

The rebound pic: Most Booksters return to their prerelationship pic. It's a way of saying, "Hey, I'm back where I started, and

that's not so bad." But why not jazz the pic up a bit? Give yourself a Photoshop tan or a Microsoft Paint moustache (guys only).

Gifts: You might as well keep them. We have it on good authority that they will be convertible to class B shares of Facebook Corp. stock when the Team goes public around fall 2009. (Special triple-secret hint: Amass the toilet paper.)

Photo albums with couple shots: There's not much you can do about these if you didn't post them yourself. Personally e-mailing Team Facebook (f_book@gmail.com) works if you catch them in the right mood. But on the wrong day, they'll end up featuring your breakup on the Global Feed just for yuks.

REVENGE

You've been dumped and now you want revenge. In public. Facebook-style.

Create a photo album with pics of just you and the ex. Then give it a name that damns with faint praise, like "Somewhat OK Times (All Things Considered)" or "Testing My Digicam . . . No Real Memories Here."

Offer your ex a humiliating gift, like the breath mints or the homeless man's hat.

"Arctic Chill" flavor

flies

Have a pal agree to a revealing friend detail request: "We went to school together, a school which was also attended by noted d-bag Anthony Finn." "We met at the birthday party of Jeanne Melvin (a whore)."

The Chinese character for revenge combines the minor characters for sword and lotus blossom. In other words, you achieve revenge through strength/sword and deviousness/lotus blossom. Sleep with your ex's sister.

A quickie marriage isn't a terrible way to inspire jealousy. The best places to troll for a Facebook spouse of convenience are the groups "Facebook is literally my last chance at happiness" and "This particular group on Facebook is literally my last chance at happiness."

TRUE-LIFE BREAKUP TALES

"A guy I didn't know asked me to be in a relationship. It was creepy at first—he didn't have any pictures or friends and his address was listed as 'the darkness.' But I figured, 'What the hey?' I didn't have anything going on, and I'd already forged some pretty close friendships on the Mr. Big vs. Aidan group. Maybe this was my chance at happiness. . . . Turns out a Performance Artist had created a fauxfile for the Devil, and he needed a girl with black hair and huge boobs for his bride. We broke up a couple of months later when he moved to South Carolina."

"I had accepted the fact that we were broken up. But I refused to take down my profile pic, the one with us together in Prague in front of all this, like, architecture. I'm not that photogenic a guy (because of my muscles), and this was a rare good shoot of me. Also, I looked extra buff in the Eastern European sun. She kept pestering me about it, I guess since she thought I was stalking her or something. Even though it was just cause I'm really vain. . . . Eventually, she got a nose job and left Facebook for an online network exclusively dedicated to publicists."

"I had these two friends, let's call them Chuck and Chelsea, who were dating for about six months. They had just reached that, you know, comfort stage where they'd memorized each other's birthmarks and knew their mothers' maiden names. Anyway, completely out of the Facebook blue, they broke up. (Probably rooted in Chuck's excessive fascination with Wii culture.) The thing was, neither wanted to be the first to change their status back to single. It was a game of breakup chicken.

"I think they liked the image more than the reality of it, the way we all feel about biofuels. . . . They eventually got married to other people, but kept their Facebook relationship alive. I've heard from a mutual friend that Chuck will eventually 'explain' to his kids that Chelsea died many years ago and he's kept the relationship as a Buddhist tribute."

"I go through a lot of breakups, probably because I keep picking up guys at conventions for converted gays. Anyway, to cope, I never accept or reject any friend requests I get—I just store them up on my homepage. That way, when I get dumped, I can nix like fifteen friends at the same time. I just wish Team Facebook would make friend rejections more emphatic, like include a jarring 'wah-wah' sound, or maybe shut down their profile for a day."

CHUCK AND CHELSEA

ASK THE MORALIST

Q. *Is it okay to break up with someone by changing your relationship status to single and just letting her figure it out?*

A. No.

Q. *What if I send her a thoughtful message, too? Is that enough?*

A. No.

Q. *Okay, how about a thoughtful message, a sincere gift, and a comforting wall post?*

A. Still no.

Q. *One more shot: What about all of the above, plus I let her ritualistically remove twenty of my friends so I appear somewhat less popular?*

A. Totally fine.

facebook
etiquette

Once you've joined up, Facebook soon resembles the sitting room in a posh country club: The mood appears relaxed and affable, yet it is undergirded by a thousand unspoken customs and mores. One inappropriate lunge for the sandwich tray, and your racquet privileges shall be revoked for a fortnight and two.

Much of this chapter will seem harsh, antique, draconian. Welcome to Rudy Giuliani's Ameriχa. Rules beget freedom.

Friending

A YOUNGER SIBLING

Conferring your friendship on another Bookster is the greatest gift you can give (other than the limited-edition Two Dicks in a Box). Who deserves it?

TO FRIEND OR NOT TO FRIEND

A younger sibling still in high school: Reject. Don't relent to their feeble grasps for straws of coolness. After all, you had to work long and hard to sit at the collegian's table. Not to mention a single friendship with a thirteen-year-old makes you a Creepster in nine states.

A popular professor: Accept, then delete. He's got a blog, a band, a British-y accent, and a yen for some undergrad street cred. So he'll be in a state of grade-inflating euphoria when notified that you've accepted him. And should he chance upon the deletion, you can blame it on Internet phenomena he's too old to fathom ("I think a meme unfriended us.").

A former significant other: Accept. Your ex loses the game of relationship chicken by requesting you—that is, unless he or she is now dating someone much hotter. In which case you should replace your profile pic with a photo of a drooping flower as a sign of defeat.

Someone you know who works for Facebook: Request. In fact, request, and then remove, and then request again, just for added emphasis. These people are the very arbiters of friendship in a friendship-based economy; you need them, Sammy Glick.

Someone you don't know with the same last name as you: Reject. Facebook is no place for primitive tribalism. If Hillary Rodham Clinton and Bill Clinton aren't friends, you shouldn't be linked to eighth cousins on the Lipschitz side.

A Friend Whore: Reject. But don't judge too quickly—he or she may be genuinely popular or just in an especially large choir. Reject with a polite note if the Friend Whore is also your mom.

INVITATIONS

Inviting holdouts was a popular way of accruing friends back when the Book had roughly the same mass appeal as floppy disks. These days, it's a crass way of exposing someone's simplicity—like offering a ride in your Ferrari to an Amish guy in exchange for his beets.

Rule: Do not invite anyone to join the Book, unless he or she . . .

1) has spent the last two years in a coma or watching Kielowski's *Decalogue*.

2) has been trying to start a rival site where people can also befriend farm animals.

3) is a cult member and/or Vice President of the United States.

4) is Mark Zuckerberg (so he knows you appreciate his great site).

FRIEND PRUNING

Twice a year or so, you need to trim your friend hedge. Aim to send 5 percent of your list into the friend trashcan. But you can't unfriend someone just because you don't like her anymore. Falling out is for baby teeth and fat kids on the teacups ride. You can, however, unfriend people for these other reasons:

- They joined a gang.
- They got kicked out of a gang.

COACH STANTON

A BRIEF HISTORY OF A FRIEND LIST: FEATURING BILLY O'GRADY

NOVEMBER 2004, FRIEND COUNT 3 — High school in rural Iowa—friends only with his sister, Coach Stanton, and a tractor.

JUNE 2005, FRIEND COUNT 4 — Persuades his first love, Judy Sweettree, to join. But she's corrupted by the Web and sent to a nunnery that doesn't even have its own network.

SEPTEMBER 2005, FRIEND COUNT 356 — Freshman week at a major East Coast University—a veritable all-you-can-eat buffet of friending. New friends include his entire hallway, social psych section, and the Cannabis Appreciation Society.

MARCH 2005, FRIEND COUNT 879 — Problems a-brewing when Billy wakes up to find he's friends with the entire women's rugby team and has angry wall posts from most of the men's forensics team.

OCTOBER 2006, FRIEND COUNT 245 — The Great Sophomore Friend Purge—back to sanity. Billy takes comfort in the certainty that he is more purging than purged.

MARCH 2007, FRIEND COUNT 7,654 — Billy leaves school to focus on his Cranberries tribute band. One of their covers is sampled by a popular R&B impresario, leaving Billy flooded with friend requests. He accepts only those from girls named Audrey with lip rings.

JANUARY 2008, FRIEND COUNT 0 — Billy leaves Facebook as part of a bid to eliminate his carbon footprint.

DECEMBER 2008, FRIEND COUNT 18 — President-elect Paul disproves global warming. Billy scrambles to regain his friend count, but in vain, as most of his friends have moved to Mexico.

THE SQUEEZE-PIC (N): TWO FACES, ONE FRAME, ZERO ADMIRERS

I first saw her at a party. Not the fun kind of party, the kind that nominates Mike Huckabee. This was the kind where everybody's an intern and nobody's really gotten over the end of *Arrested Development*.

She was standing in a corner, nursing her potatotini. She had the quiet dignity of a Vermeer maiden, the gentle gilt tresses of a cherub, and the lithe, inevitable movements of a Chuck-E-Cheese animatron. When she smiled at me, I heard a choir of angels sing the most ethereal crunk anthem any DJ had ever layered.

Did I dare approach her? I started out, but then the local darts champion leaned into her ear and I felt as hopeless as Mr. PC in those commercials with the homeless kid. I ran to the bar to take a shot of courage. But by the time I turned around—just like Perez Hilton's journalistic ethics—she was gone.

Flash forward to a dorm room in America. The monitor shone through the cold spring night as I disconsolately browsed the Book. And then suddenly, in that rhapsody of clicks, there she was, smiling that wry, world-weary-but-forgiving smile—think Jon Stewart after the perfect Cheney-gaffe alley-oop.

Now was my chance to serenade, and the Facebook poke was my guitar. But wait. There was another person in that squeeze-pic—a very different kind of person. A sea monster kind of person. The kind of person who looks like she designed her own major in womyn's herstory. The kind of person who looks like vomit.

Which one was Maggie Donovan? Could it be that the love of my life was sharing a scorpion bowl with a violator of Facebook's cardinal rule: *Never, under any circumstances, post a profile pic with a member of the same sex who's hotter than you?*

No. Impossible. With all the resolution of a sports hero injecting a growth hormone, I extended my virtual finger and poked.

Well, I overestimated the Facebook community, and before I knew it, the sea monster had me embroiled in a harassment lawsuit. I guess I should be happy in the end, because it was kind of a landmark case or whatever. But the original girl's name was Stephanie—which I hate—and we went on a few dates and she turned out to be totally clingy.

WALL POST VS. MESSAGE QUIZ

Decide whether each of the following communiqués should be a wall post or a message. Remember, wall posts are what you want everyone to see; messages are what you only want your friend, the Team, and the Russian press to see. Answers on page 182.

Thank god I'm back in America. Prague was a total sketchapalooza. Still can't tell if I got my nose pierced or stabbed. Cocktails?!

Kirsten, I'm so glad you're finally on Facebook! Here's your first wall post!

Happy birthday!! It's so ironic that the Witness Protection Program assigned you a birthday on the very day Jimmy the Mace was released. What are the odds? BTW, I heard you're in Phoenix this week! Um, hello? Cocktails?!

Erica, will you do the honor of marrying me? Before you answer, keep in mind I can only afford a Second Life wedding right now. But take a look at how many gifts I have in my giftbox. That's right, baby—it can all be yours.

My friend the IRS agent says you hooked up with a pug-fugly girl last night. Or at least somebody with Social Security #160-53-2390 did.

So I know we're not actually in a relationship per se and we just met in psych class and you're into girls and whatnot. But I've been telling my family back in Oklahoma that I've been dating someone named Phoebe, and they finally got a computer and my brother Ames is signing up for the Book right after the first snowfall. So, what would it take to make us happen? None of this open relationship stuff neither.

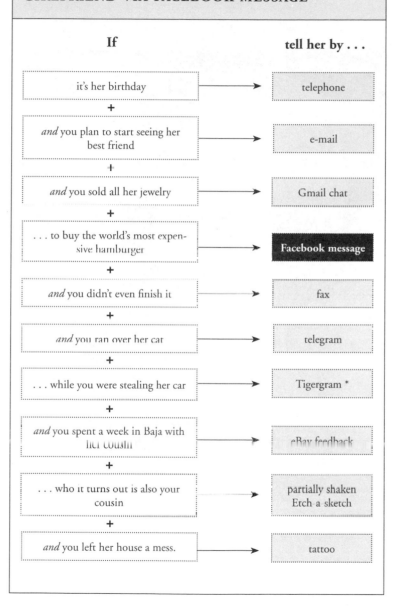

WHEN YOU CAN BREAK UP WITH YOUR GIRLFRIEND VIA FACEBOOK MESSAGE

If → **tell her by . . .**

If	tell her by . . .
it's her birthday	telephone
and you plan to start seeing her best friend	e-mail
and you sold all her jewelry	Gmail chat
. . . to buy the world's most expensive hamburger	**Facebook message**
and you didn't even finish it	fax
and you ran over her car	telegram
. . . while you were stealing her car	Tigergram *
and you spent a week in Baja with her cousin	eBay feedback
. . . who it turns out is also your cousin	partially shaken Etch a sketch
and you left her house a mess.	tattoo

* (a new service from Siegfried and Roy)

Do Nots

PLEASE, JUST DON'T, OKAY?

SARA JOHNSON

*There are infinitely many ways to go wrong on the Book. Borges's
library devotes an entire wing to Bookish mishaps. What follows
is but a grain of sand on Facebook Blunder Beach (located on the
Jersey Shore).*

PHOTO-TAGGING HORROR STORIES

Dave Hill (Palo Alto, CA): "I'd called in sick to go to the Angels game, and the next thing you know someone has tagged a photo of me hitting a grand slam. What an embarrassment! I play for the Dodgers."

Karen Stein (Facebook): "Imagine how embarrassing it was when people at the Camp saw photos of me at MySpace HQ. Plus, a lot of what goes on there is pretty NSFW."

Sara Johnson (Topeka, KS): "In my friend's album 'Circus Fun 2008' he accidentally tagged a bearded lady as me. I didn't say anything, though, because her beard was shorter and thinner than mine."

Arthur Dumont (Chicago, IL): "Someone tagged a picture of a bear as me. A bear. To be fair, it was wearing my baseball hat."

Helene Sturm (no network): "The number of photos in which you're tagged is the closest thing Facebook has to an absolute coolness rating. So I'll take any tag. A cloud, a piece of bread, a surfboard—as long as it's not fat."

GROUPTHINK

Choose your groups with the same care you put into choosing a college, fraternal society, or Free Sub Club. In other words, don't join any of the following:

Over-adminned groups. Any group that has more than twenty admins, usually people who are simply seeking the validation and magisterium of titles. Admins with honorifics like "Sergeant Pink Pants" or "Official Crasian Liaison" are just bad people.

Lost-cell-phone groups. Not only snub the group, but delete this person from your life. Go on, she doesn't know how to find you now anyway.

Nerd groups. Specifically groups that glorify nerdiness, like "People who have a Fibonacci number of friends" or "There is a boatload of Masonic imagery in The Magic Flute."

RIP groups. The problem with these is that you have to leave them at some point, exposing the exact moment when you stop honoring a person's memory. We have it on good authority that the Team will soon introduce an official Yahrzeit ceremony for each Facebook memorial, allowing it to dissolve tastefully.

MOST COMMON FAUX PAS

Misleading relationship-like photo. You may not be alone with a member of the opposite sex in your profile pic unless it's your significant other. No exceptions. Not even if you've totally got a Jim-and-Pam thing going on.

Chain-letter wall posts. The mark you leave on walls must be as unique as your dental work. If you're hit by the sexy truck, keep it in park.

Pointing out spelling and grammatical errors. There's a reason the Team banned William Safire before the launch.

Inviting friends to an event honoring POWs. Fine in theory, but keep in mind that unresponsive guests will be listed as "Missing in Action."

Concocting groups as a trap. The fact that you come from a small town doesn't give you the right to start a "Small Town Dwellers Megagroup" and friending everyone who joins.

Purging wall posts. Your wall is like the autograph page in your yearbook: It's technically yours, but tearing pages out will win you a disapproving glare from Principal Zuck.

Poking. Like, in general.

Dismissive Friend Detail requests. If you're going to add details, don't do it to distance yourself from someone you've already accepted. You can't have it both ways. And for god's sake, none of this "We met through a friend." We all know everybody we know through a friend (Jesus).

Looking For "Networking." This shouldn't be an option except on Facebook for BlackBerry, which, in turn, shouldn't exist.

WHEN IS FACEBOOK STALKING STALKING?

Facebook Stalking (okay)	Regular Stalking (not okay)
Studying the stalkee's calendar of events and showing up casually at one	Studying the stalkee's calendar of events and showing up stalkingly at one
Reading a book among the stalkee's Favorites	Making a feature-length movie out of that book and dedicating it to the stalkee
Speculating who the stalkee might have dated based on their friends and wall posts	Speculating in corn futures so you can one day be rich enough to woo the stalkee
Friending the stalkee's friends	Friending the stalkee's physician
Subtly tailoring your profile to be more amenable to the stalkee	Subtly tailoring your brain to be more amenable to the stalkee

ASK THE MORALIST

Q. *Am I allowed to repress changes from my News Feed?*

A. No more than a newspaper can sit on a story about a cottaging politician.

Q. *Okay, fine. But what if I accepted an invitation to a really exclusive party, and the host wouldn't want my other friends to know they were excluded. Isn't that more of a gray area?*

A. . . .

Q. Hello?

A. *Listen, do whatever you want.*

CONFUCIUS ON FACEBOOK

- A man who desires 10,000 friends first must have one.
- Your app should not ask "Where have I been?" but "Where have I yet to go?"
- He pokes hardest who pokes least.
- The greatest truth is not in a man's profile, but in his password.
- Is a group without members still a group? . . . Yes.
- The gods' Favorite Quote is silence.
- First, stalk thyself.

springtime
for
facebook

{the early days}

Facebook wasn't built in a day. Not even in Internet time, where a day is 25 hours. Rather, it emerged gradually from lava, like the liquid-alloy T-1000 in *Terminator 2: Judgment Day*. But its true greatness was present right from the start. In fact, the original home page had a big quote that read "This thing's gonna be great!"

Three Origin Myths

I. THE OLD MAN AND THE Z

It was snowing in Cambridge, and Zuckerberg's sandal-clad feet were frostbitten. A long night of coding lay ahead of him. By the next morning, he had to program a computer to beat *Oregon Trail* as the carpenter. Without cheat codes.

On his way to Olde Widener Library, young Zuckerberg came upon a mysterious man. Stranger than most men, the mysterious man wore two monocles and two beards. His pipe blew smoke in the shape of ampersands.

"Spare a bite to eat?" the mysterious man asked.

All Zuckerberg had was half an Odwalla bar. But he gave it up just the same. (It tasted like crap.)

"Thank you, kind sir. And in return I will tell you a riddle. What kind of book has no pages?"

"I've got it: an online facebook!" replied Zuckerberg.

"What a dull-witted response. I'm ashamed to have taken your charity," said the mysterious man, casting the Odwalla bar to the ground. "In fact, I question whether you should be in college at all."

And the mysterious man was never heard from again. Until he joined Facebook in 2006.

II. REDEMPTION

Zuckerberg gets in trouble for using the student body's ID photos on a home-brewed version of HOT or NOT?.

The disciplinary committee of Harvard College met in the basement of the rarely frequented Museum of Diseases and Flowers. To get to their hallowed chambers, one must pass through a narrow corridor lined with the busts of famed expellees William Randolph Hearst, Ted Kennedy, and Archibald Brocke (who was, coincidentally, decapitated later in life). The room itself was bare, except for a few items of furniture and a used cyclotron.

Zuckerberg sat on the contrition bench wearing the traditional Humility Robe and Humbling Hat.

The chairperson spoke with the gravity of a Supreme Court Justice, because in fact he was one (Antonin Scalia).

"Harvard would prefer on the whole not to expel you. It's bad for our U.S. News rankings and, frankly, unsporting. What we do ask for is penance. Usually in the form of cash, occasionally stocks or other rated securities. In your case, though, being a member of the trade class, we'll ask you to render a service instead. We want you to use your computer programming skills for good, not prank. Members of the committee, any ideas?"

"An artificially intelligent registrar?"

"A cafeteria menu widget?"

"An online facebook?"

"Well, choose whichever one tickles your hacker's bone and get back to us in a month."

Zuckerberg didn't get back to them and so he was expelled from Harvard (for one day).

III. DORM ROOM FOLLIES

Just a typical Saturday night. Zuckerberg and his roommates sat on the floor of their dorm room playing a drinking game.

It involved flipping a quarter onto a mousetrap while constantly high-fiving each other.

"I've got a better idea," the popped-collared one said. "Let's look through the freshman facebook and pick out the girls we'd murder, marry, or maim."

"But those photos are so out-of-date," replied Jason. "Ever heard of a little thing called the freshman fifteen?"

"Not to mention the sophomore seven and the junior nose job," chimed in another Jason.

"If only there were a way to put these photos online and make ten billion dollars," Zuckerberg thought to himself in a corner.

And the rest is on Wikipedia.

INTERVIEW WITH THE NON-CS ROOMMATE

This is another legend. Zuckerberg had four roommates, three of whom were into CS; a fourth favored poetry. We met at a local Starbucks.

(INTERVIEWER'S NOTE: HE COUGHED EVERY TIME I MENTIONED THE WORDS FACEBOOK, ZUCKERBERG, AND ENJAMBMENT.)

Q. *How did it feel being roommates with the very people who would become the core of Team Facebook?*

A. I mean, whatever. Who needs Facebook when you have real books? People think that's a rhetorical question, but I tell you, it's not.

Q. *But surely if you had an even marginal knowledge of programming, web design, or anything remotely related to the world of commerce and men's affairs, they would have brought you on the Team.*

A. Give me a quote from Auden. Any quote. I'll tell you which poem and a fun fact about it. Slam. Dunk.

Q. *And of course if you had been involved from the beginning, you'd be rich by now. Free to spend all day reading.*

A. I've memorized more sonnets than Team Facebook combined. Combined.

Q. *Did you learn anything from your roommates?*

A. Let me tell you a little story about a man called J. Keats. He was writing immortal poems when Mr. Zuckerberg was taking Poetry and Literature for Science Majors—a mandatory class. Now who's the wunderkind?

Q. *Do you have a Facebook profile?*

A. Did Wordsworth have a Game Boy?

Q. *Regrets?*

A. Only that I didn't think of the Milton quote-of-the-day app first.

(INTERVIEWER'S NOTE II. ON THE WAY OUT, HE DIPPED A HANDFUL OF STIRRING RODS IN CREAM AND PUT THEM IN HIS POCKET.)

THE UR-FACEBOOK (AN APPRECIATION)

May also be called The Pig Book, The Meat Menu, The Fresh Face Free Fun Folio, The Peepster's Pamphlet

Old-timey facebooks had neat features, apps, bells, whistles, and shenanigans aplenty. We should appreciate that which is old, before it is really old. *See following page for visual.*

can't be updated, no
flowing with the trends

Ashley Cox
Sarasota, FL

Patrick Cutrone
Irvine, CA

Shai Daniels
Alexandria, VA

see how your
friends look
with glasses,
cigars, head
wounds

Amanda Davis
Cleveland, OH

Donna Dean
St. George, MD

James Dietrich
Fellashioe, PA

Larissa Donisov
Murmansk, Russia

Ana Eisenberg
Poughkeepsie, NY

Joseph Elias
Honolulu, HI

Sabrina V. Fox
Durham, NC

John Frederick
Concord, MA

Charles Girard
New York, NY

Jennifer Goose
San Diego, CA

J. Mortimer Gyllenhaal Jr.
East Haven, KA

Angela Hays
Helena, M.T.

paper will outlast the inevitable
Internet Superworm (albeit not
regular bookworms)

if one of your classmates
becomes a celebrity, will
be slightly more valuable

Julia Heiser
Birmingham, MI

Karla Hendricks
Hatch, NM

James Holmes
Somerville, MA

Samuel Horvath
New York, NY

David Kaplan
San Antonio, TX

Vanessa Kay
Syracuse, NY

Andrew Kim
Durango, CO

Henry Kingfisher
Memphis, TN

Kevin Larynx
Seaside Height, NJ

Brandon Lester
Weston, CT

Corynn Levin
Philadelphia, PA

Lucy Lightman
Portland, OR

Jeremy Louis
Culver City, CA

Alice Martinez
Flagstaff, AZ

Jessica Mason
Grayling WI

Phillip McGettigan
Newton, MA

THE UR-FACEBOOK

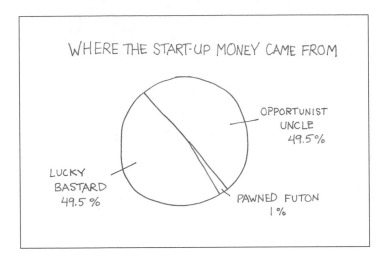

WHERE THE START-UP MONEY CAME FROM

OPPORTUNIST
UNCLE
49.5%

LUCKY
BASTARD
49.5%

PAWNED FUTON
1%

EARLY IDEAS

The first draft of Beethoven's Fifth had a bunch of superfluous power chords. We should judge genius by the final version only.

Alternate names:
- FacePlace
- PalPlanet
- Super-Friends
- BudBonanza
- AmigoVille
- Bonanza!

Alternate color schemes:
- A slightly warmer blue
- A bluer blue
- Blonde

Alternate distribution mechanisms:
- Newsletter   • Zine   • Kiosk   • Course pack

Alternate marketing scheme:

Many scholars believe the key to Facebook's success was its initial localization at Harvard. This gave the site a preppy, gated-community feel and allowed the Team to work out the kinks in a live beta. But that "strategy" may have just been a happy accident. Recent evidence shows the Team planned to go global during week two with a massive international spam and media blitz. To get the word out, they went so far as to hire out-of-work circus performers to roam (or, in one case, hop) around college campuses. However, the promotions manager got lazy and the whole thing had to be called off. All that's left from this alternate plan is a warehouse filled with blue cotton candy mix.

THE EDENIC PERIOD

"There were three girls to every guy, and at least five guys to every girl. How is that possible? It isn't: Back then, Facebook was literally magic."

"I, like, messaged this girl 'hey,' and the next thing you know we're Book-married. Then I messaged her 'what's up,' and we had real-life sex."

"It was all so new and different. Like when Game Genie came out for Nintendo and Mega Man could shoot green. Or when you discovered that pizza parlor that sold Jolt Cola to minors."

"There was just this honesty. To learn that so many of my peers shared my passion for *The Catcher in the Rye* made me feel like I was part of something larger than myself. It was a community. Nay, it was a Facebook."

"I had mono then, and so it was a great chance to make friends without leaving my room. Then I got the mono computer virus, and I returned to a life of solitude."

"As a hipster, I finally was able to locate the one other guy who sort of liked Archers of Loaf."

"It made computers cool again. Which was great, because I own like three of 'em."

THE GOLDEN-BLUE MOMENT

A list of what Harvard students were doing at 8:04 p.m. on February 4, 2004, the moment before Facebook went live:

Farley Katz was writing a blog entry about new trends in post-reality television.

Rob Quirk was eating a choco-vanil fro-yo silently in a bathroom.

Joey Fasano was sleep-peeing.

Sarah Schweig was violently hugging a pillow sham in lieu of a human.

Andrei Nikita was crying due to boredom.

Marie Morris was terrified of her own e-mails.

Matt Swizkowski was listening to his iPod too loud in order to block out the wrath.

Nicky Silvio was buying *Magic: The Gathering* cards.

Andrew Bell was playing the Flash game *Gold Miner* rather than a brand new PS2.

Beth McMillen was photographing homeless people sarcastically.

Emily Claire was in a piano trio without a decent bassist.

Kim Wong was studying for the MCAT even though it was two years away and snowing.

Simon "Frankie" Rich was just about to sign up for Friendster.

ANOTHER PERSPECTIVE: A HARVARD PROFESSOR TALKS ABOUT WHAT IT WAS LIKE

I had no idea what this whole Friendbook thing was about. Sounded to me like a kind of videogame. Or maybe a dating system that matched you based on your preferences among the Great Books. Then I realized it was most probably a pyramid scheme.

I tried to find it on Google's search engine, but without success. It seemed Mr. Google was on a smoking break that afternoon. Next, I asked a grad student, but found him too sullen. Still have no idea what it is. Something to do with bookmaking? Heraldry? Falconry?

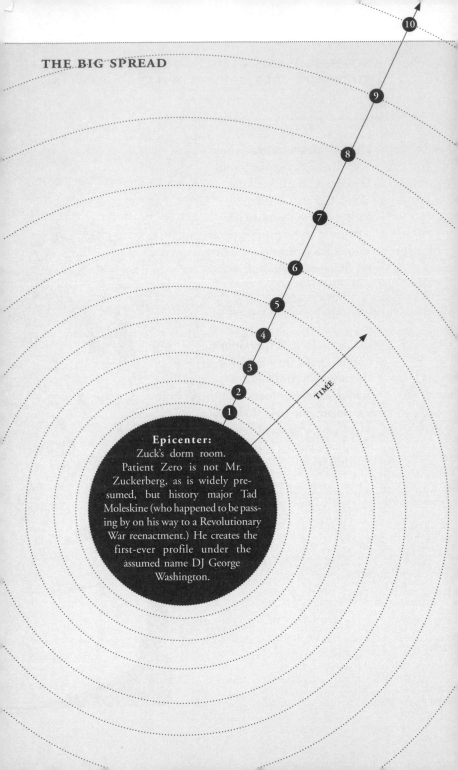

THE BIG SPREAD

TIME

1 2 3 4 5 6 7 8 9 10

Epicenter:
Zuck's dorm room. Patient Zero is not Mr. Zuckerberg, as is widely presumed, but history major Tad Moleskine (who happened to be passing by on his way to a Revolutionary War reenactment.) He creates the first-ever profile under the assumed name DJ George Washington.

1) **8:15 pm** The entryway hears about it during brain break, but the main topic of discussion is the delicious brownies; socialite Margaret Pearson is present, but she dismisses the idea as another procrastibatory Snood; the spread is set back five minutes.

2) **8:30 pm** The one CS major/jock mentions the Book in the locker room amid towel-snapping and other tomfoolery; his fellow equestrians decide to join out of gentlemanly camaraderie.

3) **8:50 pm** A student at MIT tries to join, but he can't yet; he will later go on to program the "Jennifer Aniston has sent you a message on Facebook" virus.

4) **9:15 pm** Membership reaches critical mass and the student newspaper does a story about the phenomenon with the headline "Face It: Facebook is for Book Faces, Bro."

5) **9:21 pm** Pockets of fine art majors, the super-rich, and vegans are refusing to join, but they all succumb after Friendship Friday.

6) **9:45 pm** Other Boston-area schools are added to the network, including MIT, BU, and the Boston School of Beef; members of the band Boston are also given a dispensation to join (although only Barry Goudreau takes up the offer)

7) **10:10 pm** The mid-Atlantic colleges fall next in a social-networking blitzkrieg; the militaristic metaphor is appropriate because the Naval Academy was one of them.

8) **11:15 pm** The West Coast is largely untouched by the Facebook juggernaut, until the Team hires an actual titanium juggernaut to infiltrate the UC schools.

9) **11:30 pm** The South is absorbed after the harvest comes in.

10) **11:55 pm** A UN delegate from Benin is the first foreigner to create a profile; the Security Council begins immediate deliberations over whether Facebook should be considered a sovereign entity.

THE "RIVALS"

For legal and emotional reasons, we can't get too much into the Facebook Pretenders. Basically, some Harvard students may or may not have been working on projects similar or dissimilar to Facebook while high or not high on Ivy League-ish self-delusion. The Courts and the Blogosphere will have to sort it out. (If you absolutely must know more, Google "facebook fraud sour grapes whiners abercrombie.")

Here is a totally imaginary version of what one of these Pretenders might have written in the intro to his/her memoirs:

If I Programmed It . . .

Thing is, Zuckernerd—or should I say Zuckerturd—was just a cog in my machine. An actor in my play, a serf on my manor, a backup dancer in my Britney Spears concert. The true story is that a droplet of genius accidentally rolled off my brow and onto his expectant tongue. Yeah, he's made a somewhat successful career from my droppings. But so could anyone if they stole the plot of Hamlet.

. . .

What of it that I don't know C++ or Java? And I.M. Pei might not know how to go bang-bang with a hammer. Every line of code of that Fakebook originated in my glandular system. Anyway, the real truth rests with God, Me, and Ayn Rand.

. . .

But it doesn't bother me that much anymore. I'm working on a new project that's going to make Facebook look like a shock site. I can't tell you more for obvious reasons, but let's just say it involves dating and surprises.

people of the book

As Charleton Heston might have put it, Facebook is people, you fools, it was people the whole time. And what a diverse bunch, too. You'll even find adults

SARAH YNEZ

Facebook could exist without them, but why bother? A solid meme, each and every one. Up and down the blue carpet they stroll in their minks and their top hats and their Harry Winston bejweledness. Ah, the perfume of bright young things, the famous and the dangerous.

SUPERLATIVES

Most friends: Dave Zarkoff, 823,192. Dave, a software engineer and Digg digger, hacked into the Facebook mainframe and gave himself an artificially high friend count. The number is an allusion to the mathematician Ramanujan's favorite number (because it says something ribald in Hindi when you enter it upside down on a calculator). In reality, Dave has about 8 friends, and that includes some children.

Most wall posts: Clara Banksy, 35,182. In an attempt to lure endless birthday wishes, Clara changed her date of birth to the current date every day for two years. She got greedy when she tried to pull off Sweet Sixteen and Naughty Nineteen on consecutive days.

Oldest member: Roger Crosby, age 102. Fun fact: Had Facebook been around in the 1920s, Roger would have used his profile as a kind of online speakeasy.

Youngest member: Sarah Ynez, age eleven months. While you technically must be thirteen to join Facebook, who could say no to a hipster baby?

Most record-breaking profile pic: Tom Shulte. Smoking 101 cigarettes while he and his Siamese twin unicycle the Hoover Dam, each wearing a beard of bees.

Most poked: Ross Graff, 6.4×10^5. According to doctors, this many physical pokes would lead to massive renal failure.

CELEBRITIES WITH SECRET PROFILES

- ★ John Mellencamp
- ★ Anderson Cooper
- ★ Dennis Kucinich's wife
- ★ Scottie Pippen
- ★ The dog from *Beethoven*

IN THEIR OWN WORDS

Sara Friedman, *Portraitist of the Book:* I like painting random people, and you see a lot of random people on the Book. Right now I'm working on a series called "You Didn't Expect *Me* to be Wearing a Tie." During my Yellow Period, I painted frat dudes who had either spilled beer on their shirts or contracted jaundice.

Bella Arnofsky, *Sociologist of the Book:* I'm writing my PhD thesis on "Facebook Friendship in the Post-Gen-4-iPod World." Did you know being Facebook friends doesn't necessarily mean you're friends in the real world? Fascinating. Also, you can be "married" to someone without a legal certificate.

Dave Evans—Utica, New York—231 friends—Pink Floyd—*Shawshank Redemption*—spring break in Prague—summer internship at Lehman Brothers.

ARTHUR GELFMAN
Rain Man of the Book

Paul Portnoy, *"Freakonomist" of the Book:* I don't like the term Freakonomist. It's not like I *exclusively* study the wage differentials of bearded ladies. Taking my cue from Steven Levitt, I post notes with simple questions about everyday topics, but related to the Book. For instance, what factors predict how many friends you have? Turns out the surest indication of popularity is having a name that evokes a beloved celebration, like Sam Christmas or Kelly Birthday. Or what's the relationship between the number of words in your profile and obesity? Here's a hint: It's the opposite of what you think.

Roger Ute, *Talent Agent of the Book:* Searching MySpace for talent is like going to an orphanage to adopt. All the kids are trying too hard, and the really talented ones already have agents/parents. On Facebook, I get a candid look at the rosy-cheeked cheerleader who might end up the next Jenna Jameson. Or the neighborhood fat kid who could some day be the fat guy on *SNL*.

Danielle Lindh, *Historian of the Book:* I'm working on a three-volume history of the Facebook Generation titled *Profiles in Procrastination*. The thesis of the book is that Facebook will usher in a new era of peace and prosperity, which will come to a gruesome end when apps become self-aware.

Colin Faust, *Private Investigator of the Book:* Old broads hire me to check out their daughters' boyfriends. I've uncovered a few who were cheating, but even more who were into ultimate Frisbee.

Sean Hamilton, *Evangelist of the Book:* It's not like the Team *needs* me to spread the good news about the Book. I just love doing it. I walk the roads, highways, alleyways, gangways, main drags, and minor shortcuts of this great nation, a laptop under one arm and a smile under the other. Still, a lot of people haven't heard of the Book. Particularly in the Bebo Belt. I've never received a restraining order that I didn't want.

Gemma O'Grady, *Social Gadfly of the Book:* Facebook contributes to the dilution of friendship. So my hobby is finding random pairs of friends in my networks (Colgate, San Diego) and getting them to admit they don't really like each other by barraging them with messages and wall posts.

Dan, *Hobo of the Book:* I was kicked off the Book for graffiti that the copper buttons called "too filthy for the Internet." Nowadays I wander into Internet cafes hoping some Richie Rockefeller has left his account open so I can use up his online do-re-mi. Nothin' like a game of Scrabulous to warm this old hobo's heart.

Copernicus C, *Messiah of the Book:* I've been called to lead all these sinners out of Sodom-dot-com and into the promised land, a social-networking Valhalla, where people may post their favorite psalms and least favorite rap lyrics. Wake up and smell the JavaScript!

Elizabeth Beaver, *Exile of the Book:* I was part of the great raunchy name pogrom of July 2006 that also victimized Julius Putz, Harry Felashio, and Gaylord Belcher. Our names are real, and so is our hurt.

BEAUTY QUEENS SCANDALIZED BY THE BOOK

It seems every recent Miss Teen USA has gotten into trouble as a result of Facebook photo albums. A random sampling:

Miss Teen South Carolina's profile pic showed her bottomless on a topless beach.

Miss Teen Nebraska's profile pic depicted her riding a dog like a horse.

Miss Teen Utah was listed in a relationship with Mr. Teen USA (a spokesman for the Young Aryan Nation).

Miss Teen Hawaii's profile pic showed her holding cans of beer in her sash like a bandolier.

Miss Teen Arizona's profile pic showed her using her tiara to tap a keg.

MISS TEEN MINNESOTA

OTHER PEOPLE SCANDALIZED BY THE BOOK

Alex Smatterling, 25, clerked for a judge on the Second Circuit Court of Appeals. For his profile pic, he had the bailiff take a photo of him in judge's robes, sitting on the bench and brandishing a noose. Little did  Alex know it's a serious offense to impersonate a federal judge. He was executed with the very same noose.

Dirk Chestnut wrote music reviews for tastemaking hipster webzine Pitchfork Media. Known as a snob among snobs, he once criticized sacred cow Sufjan Stevens for composing a song in C major. But some bloggers got hold of his Facebook profile and discovered his favorite music included Billy Joel and the Eagles (*not* the German power-punk collective). He was summarily written off as a "fraudster" despite pleas that his selections were intended as "hyper-ironic performance art."

Arturas Rivnunkas lost the Latvian presidency in a landslide after voters discovered that one of his friends had "thrown a sheep" at him, a traditional symbol of emasculation.

James Grandnaught was an analyst at Goldman Sachs. He was fired for writing a *Jerry Maguire*-esque rant about the soulless-ness of banking and "modern America™" in his About Me. The bank also expressed concern about the sheer number of costume parties he was attending.

Lisa White's profile clearly exposed her as a Friend Whore, which made things kind of awkward in her job as a nun.

Frank Phelan lost his associate professorship in the classics when the chair of the department discovered he had received a lot of wall posts from preteens and postmodernists.

Harvey Sturm, 26, hotshot CIA agent, posted a list of top secret codenames underneath Interests. The government was not amused, and he had his poison-dart cane confiscated.

HARVEY STURM

Apple-brand doily

SOME GRANDMAS

Ginny Andrews

I'm not your ordinary granny.

Most old ladies, when they get to that certain age postmeno-pause and precorpse, give up on life. They take off their shoes, lie down in the coffin, and distribute their remaining knick-knacks to the grandkids. Then the smallest grandkid slams the lid shut, and that's that.

But not me. Like a Japanese soldier on one of those islands, I'm going to fight to the end.

So when I read about Facebook in *Reader's Digest*, I just had to try it. It's not a regular book like you'd think. It's a site on the Internet's worldwide web, and you can visit it using an ordinary computer box. (So of course you also need electricity.) On this so-called "web site," you put up a photo of yourself and make friends. Not robot friends, but actual people, like you. Anyway, the article said that if seniors use it for five minutes a day, they'll ward off dementia for another week. Why, that would almost carry me through to March!

Abigail Monroe

"What are some of your favorite movies?" the boy asked.

It sounded like he was flirting with me. "Young person, don't you know I'm old enough to be your widow?"

"But, ma'am, it's for your profile."

My cheeks turned Maimie Eisenhower red.

"Hmmm. My favorite movies. Let me think. Why, I do enjoy that young William Ferrell. He reminds me of my son-in-law, the tax attorney. I think it's their *joie de vivre*."

"So, maybe *Anchorman*?"

"No, I don't like his comedies."

"Do you have any favorite books, then?"

"Anything about cats I love equally well. Even that awful *Sharpe's Guide to Taxidermy*."

"Or how about we just upload a photo? We can take one using the webcam."

"No, I'm afraid I'm not the great beauty I was at twenty-two.

"Did you know Zbigniew Brzezinski once wrote me a dirty limerick? Translating from the Polish, it begins—"

But the boy had already left. Just like Zbig.

Mildred Cook

What does a grandma need with the Internet anyway? I've already got a gaggle of cats and a giggle of grandchildren. What use is Google? All of my recipes are stored neatly on 3x5 index cards in a squirrel-shaped box, thank you very much. And the only "E-mail" I ever want to receive is my weekly letter from Evelyn.

But Facebook piqued my interest. I first heard about it from Marjorie. She sits to my immediate left in the knitting circle. (Well, she used to sit two seats to my left before Gertie and Partridge died in that medication mix-up.) And she's a gabber, that Marje. Always prattling on about what she read in the magazines. One day it's Iraq, the next it's Iranian supermodel Cameron Alborzian. What a cracker!

Anyway, she said she uses Facebook to spy on her grandkids. I don't mean "spy" in the Tom Clancy sense, but more the Graydon Carter/Kurt Andersen sense. That is, all in good, clean fun.

So I decided to take a little sneak-a-peek myself.

It turns out my grandson Zander's interests include procrastination and sleeping. No wonder he's always so droopy-eyed. And I thought it was the candy!

And I was shocked to learn my granddaughter Felicity is

married to another girl. But Marje explained it to me. At Smith we used to call it a LUMP (lesbian until marriage proposal).

SOME GRANDPAS

Jack Smoltz

In the army, we didn't have no Facebook. All we had was a big jar filled with the dog tags of our fallen brothers. One guy got a tattoo of his favorite whore's face on his arm. But it was hardly something you'd put in a book.

Irwin Karnofsky

Why can't there be a Facebook for racehorses? You could call it the Ponybook or Racebook or Mr. Karnofsky's Social Networking Website for Thoroughbreds. What do I need a Facebook for my human friends? If they're not dead, they're at the racetrack. Or maybe a Facebook for Social-Security checks.

Sal Boozer

Eh, Facebook Schmacebook. Give me a website where you can read about prison riots in real time. Now that would be something I'd put some pennies into.

Aaron Gray

I admit it. I'm just on Facebook to ogle the coeds. Can't do that safely anymore except in front of a computer screen. I used to dress up as a homeless man and hang around campus to survey the ladies. But I got in trouble because some prude claimed that wasn't behavior appropriate for a professor.

JAR OF DOG TAGS

TWO HARVARD ALUMNI REMINISCE

Facebook is played out, man. It's so October 2007.

Yeah, Facebook reeks of 10/07.

Oil hits $90 a barrel, Facebook peaks, and The Darjeeling Limited *opens to mixed reviews. Fantastic. Let's move on to November already.*

And I'm not player-hating 'cause I'm jealous or anything.

No. Of course not. That would be Yale-ish.

I mean, remember the last Internet bubble? One day you were shopping for castles in Tuscany, the next a time-share on a space station.

So what if Facebook is valued at 15 billion dollars? All the 15 billion dollars in the world won't buy you happiness.

Or true friendship.

Or the sweet stink of poverty.

Paper money, it's all paper money.

Give me gold any day of the week.

Hell, I'd take silver.

I'm not saying it J'd the S, though.

Way too cliché.

But everyone's started apping out their profiles like a humanimal gets body mods.

MySpace is looking austere in comparison.

Amherst austere.

Yup. And who wants to be on a social network with your mom? I mean specifically your mom, Mrs. Partridge. She's kind of like Martha Stewart without the affection.

Tell me about it. Hospital corners every day. Even after naptime.

I think Facebook should never have expanded outside of Harvard Yard.

Maybe just to add the local racquetball clubs and our sister school in Japan, Harvardojimbo.

That first glorious week, it was perfection. Why'd they get rid of Favorite Horatian Odes, anyway? Too highbrow?

Fuhgeddabout it. At the very least, they should have given us early adopters a special privilege.

An ivy border around our profile page?

Pretentious, but honest.

✔ FACEBOOK PEOPLE SCAVENGER HUNT

How many can you find? How many can you not find?

- [ ] a guy double-fisting Solo cups
- [ ] a guy single-fisting a double-barreled shotgun
- [ ] a guy just chillin' (in a giant Solo cup)
- [ ] Paul Rudd
- [ ] a guy with his arms folded and an expression of quiet insouciance on his face, like he just successfully tapped his first keg
- [ ] a completely unironic raised eyebrow
- [ ] a guy playing *Guitar Hero* while a LoLcat looks on, playing a miniature version of the game
- [ ] a guy with an honest-to-goodness handlebar moustache (we're talking worthy of a Ken Burns documentary)
- [ ] a South Dakotan
- [ ] a guy doing amateurish parkour

camp
facebook

Camp as in Anawanna, not kitsch.

Camp Facebook

The geniuses at Google wanted to design the ideal work environment for their employees. So they modeled their HQ after a college campus (specifically Stanford, a place where trees literally grow in classrooms). The employees of Facebook skew a little younger, so they decided to model their HQ off a summer camp.

A HANDY CHART

- Google: a college
- Facebook: a summer camp
- Apple: the city of the future

- Yahoo!: a carnival
- Amazon: a pinball machine
- YouTube: a tube

FRIENDSHIP AT CAMP FACEBOOK

Is everyone on Team Facebook friends? No. Like at every camp, there are five distinct cliques that can never be friends.

Hackers
Brain surgeons, fighter pilots, iron chefs—every organization has its elite force. At the Book, it's the computer programmers known as hackers—or on a giddy day, hacksters. They get personal parking spots for their hybrid cars/mopeds. Will often wear sunglasses to keep others from being blinded.

Computer Programmers
Okay, so if Hackers are the Ivy League*, then these fellows are your dependable northeastern universities: healthy endowment, groomed lawns, and a couple of famous-in-their-field names. In other words, Tufts. Yeah, they get the job done, just don't expect too much gilding or perfume. Lovable bunch, these.

Technicians
These guys are the foam on top of your beer—necessary for the full effect, but ain't gonna get you drunk/rich. So don't ask them to build the Parthenon, but feel free to request your shoes shined and the back of your neck talcumed.

Personnel
Talk slowly and use simple subject-verb-object grammar in their presence. A colorful desk toy (typically a blue paperclip attached to a yellow one) will keep them pacified and delighted. And they have their talents, too. Fred is great at shuffling cards.

Human Resources
Don't be frightened by their dead-eye gazes and bibs. But also don't *not* be frightened.

* Plus Stanford and CalTech!

143

A DAY IN THE LIFE AT CAMP FACEBOOK

7:00 **Reveille** Everyone's cell phone is synched to ring at 7 A.M. Not the chilling bugle call of *Salute Your Shorts* fame, but the comforting strums of "Ants Marching." You can grab one of the many solar-powered buses that roam the streets of Silicon Valley, or hop on your wakeboard and shimmy up the coast. Zuckerberg himself rides a limited-edition Segway that comes with a sidecar.

8:30 **Morning meeting** No business here. Zuckerberg leads a war chant ("Face to the Book to the Face to the Book, hugaz-zah!") and does a cartwheel for each billion the company is currently worth. Everyone is sitting on beanbag benches. A folk guitar appears but is rarely played.

9:00 **Activities** This is your time to program, design a gift in the arts and crafts workshop, or just be yourself. Be sure to code your 500-line minimum, though, or you might find your computer monitor "shaving creamed."

1:00 **Tetherball tourney** in the parking lot. For historical reasons, the ball has Bill Hewlett's face on it. Winner gets to tool around on the company ATV for an hour.

4:30 **Naptime** The Camp is outfitted with a series of hammocks and vertical sleeping bags (like astronauts have). But if you don't grab one quick, you'll be snoozing in the gaga pit.

7:00 **Evening activities** This is when the real work gets done. Bring your A-game and your game face and an MP3 by The Game, and stay until the job is done like the Spartan warrior you better be. Wonder why this small pack of twentysomethings is pwning the Internet? This is it: single-elimination foosball tournament.

10:00 **Story time** Luke the CTO continues his long-running saga about a computer virus that infects every website except Faccbook. This leads to Team Facebook becoming gatekeepers of the Internet and harnessing the power of the Google Stone. They all live together in a tower.

INTERVIEW WITH A NEW EMPLOYEE

Q. *Why did you want to work at Facebook?*

A. Who doesn't want to work here? It's like it's 1962, and the Beatles are looking for a computer programmer.

Q. *How did you find out you got the job?*

A. When they invited me to join the Facebook employees group. My friend who got passed up for the job received the Stinky Socks gift. And I don't mean a Facebook gift.

Q. *What was your first day like?*

A. Well, Zuckerberg enters majestically in this blue robe, and other guys are holding these torches that burn blue flames. I recall a string quartet playing selections from the Final Fantasy series.

Q. *Was there any hazing?*

A. Nah, they just fed us a lot of cereal. And some pretty obscure stuff. I had no idea the Nintendo Cereal System was still on the market.

Q. *Did you get any free stuff?*

A. Everyone gets issued a MacBook, an iPod, and a canteen. But I think the canteen is also manufactured by Apple because it's all white

NOOB

and everything you drink out of it has an apple-y aftertaste.

Q. *And what's your desk like?*

A. No, no desks at all. An interesting variety of sitting options, though, including a stand-alone bicycle seat and a bag of liquid.

Q. *So it's a high-concept workspace . . .*

A. They're trying to make us as creative as possible, and desks evoke grade school and Staples. And no ceiling either. Just cargo netting, which you're allowed, even encouraged to climb on.

Q. *Where would you work if not Facebook?*

A. I can't imagine being anywhere else. Maybe Disney World before it started getting all self-referential under Eisner.

CODING WARS

"Camp" should really be called "comp," because that's what camp is all about: competition. Once a month Camp Facebook hosts its own day of competitions. Except in keeping with the whole Web 2.0 thing, all the competitions involve programming.

000   Who can debug this JavaScript function the fastest? You'll be wearing mittens.

001   Program an app, spin around for a count of five mississippis, program an even better app.

010   Hack into a TiVo so that it can access Facebook and will only record scenes from *The Office* featuring Rainn Wilson.

011   Who can stay up the longest while still coding? (The winner is always Brett, an ex-Navy SEAL who can do no-handed push-ups.)

100   Bobbing for RAM.

CAMP FOOD

"Some hackers got hold of a soda
fountain and went crazy with it.
So now you can key in precise
soda combinations: 35% Pepsi,
15% Sierra Mist, 1% Dr. Pepper,
49% Diet Dr. Pepper. That's
called an Orkut-n-Pepsi. It's a pretty intuitive touch-screen
interface, although it gets kind of sticky. I also heard they're
working on a pizza cutter that's accurate to the nanometer."

"There's a lot of food-based bribery. Like the boss'll say 'first one
to figure out why no one on the Vassar network has friends gets
a fro-yo.' If you're lactose intolerant, you can opt for the Möbius
bacon strip, a staff favorite."

"We have Camp meals on this giant picnic table that doubles as
a boardroom table and triples as an air hockey table. It can also
be reassembled complexly to form a wicker man."

THE FACEBOOK SEAL

THE FACEBOOK CONSTITUTION

The Facebook Constitution was written in a surge of heady idealism by the founding Team members. They had just watched *Apocalypto* on DVD and wanted to engage in some kind of ritualistic blood oath. You can only find the Constitution in Zuckerberg's office (right next to the *New Yorker* cartoon) and printed on every napkin.

I. This ain't gonna be no pets.com; also, pets are forbidden at work.

II. Friendship is Facebook's friend, but Facebook is friendship's frenemy.

III. When in doubt, blue.

IV. If the code of Facebook is destroyed, check the back of this document for the good parts.

V. Sketchy before creepy, creepy before douchey, douchey before Friendster.

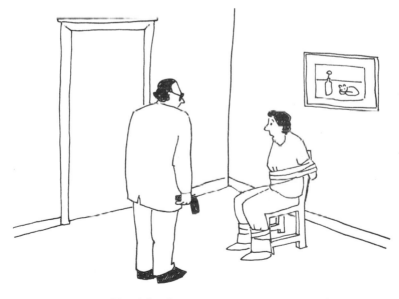

"But I thought we were Facebook friends . . ."

VI. Facebook is only as strong as the titanium alloy case that holds the primary server. Check up on it frequently.

VII. Hire no more assholes than necessary; hire as many George Soroses as possible; hire exactly one person with cat-eye contact lenses.

VIII. Never forget our humble Harvard roots.

IX. Keep on truckin' this long, strange trip.

X. We'll plan on obeying the Geneva conventions.

XI. History will judge us, unless we buy out history.com first.

FUN AND GAMES AT CAMP

"There were a bunch of investment bankers in the boardroom. And Justin is showing them these slides about the 2-to-1 philosophy—2 hours of fun for every 1 hour of work—and how we think this is a pretty awesome philosophy. And then this big fat i-banker with a monocle is like, 'Preposterous!' and a short wiry i-banker with a bow tie is like, 'You're just a bunch of kids. An outrage!" So then Justin goes, 'Oh, no, you've got it all wrong, let me prove it to you.' And a hundred balloons suddenly drop out of nowhere. And Justin says, 'Now I'll bet you this is a meeting you'll never forget,' and they all had to agree. The next day, I signed for two duffel bags of money."

SLEEPOVER

Sometimes we'll have a mandatory sleepover. You know it's coming when the Red Bull van pulls up back. (Did you know that giant can on top actually holds jet fuel?) Tastes like cough syrup, inspires like Oprah. There was this kid—didn't sleep for three days, drank some Red Bull, fell asleep, and in his dream he was able to decipher the mysteries of the human genome. So imagine what the stuff does when you mix it with Mr. Pibb!

Anyway, we just sit around in a circle with our computers and code until the work is done. Then we all head over to IHOP. Well, those of us who have day jobs there.

"Sometimes we'll just play manhunt around the office. It's simple and elegant, like Facebook itself. The jail is an actual jail in the basement. Even has an electric chair and a 'hole.'"

"Scrabulous is big, but Riskulous is bigger."

"My fave: street hockey in the parking lot. The puck is a first-gen iPod. Those things are indestructible."

"Contrary to popular belief, we don't have Star Wars Fridays, where everyone dresses up as a character from *Star Wars*. We're not just a bunch of lame fanboys. We're not Del.icio.us. That kid who wears a hood-and-cowl every day is a genuine monk."

"Paper airplanes were big circa February. Someone even devised a paper zeppelin, and it's still floating around."

"Okay, yes, we do permit ourselves the indulgence once a year of reenacting the battle for Middle Earth from *Lord of the Rings*. And, yes, we do go all out. The ring we use was forged at the Stanford cyclotron. And as it's an historically accurate reenactment, the hobbits always win. But the elves are permitted to go off script. What—do you expect to tell an elf what to do?"

A CLEANING LADY SPEAKS OUT

Every day it is the same. The floors are covered in breakfast cereal and a many-colored string. And someone has written 'Luke is a sketch-bomb' on all the whiteboards. If it is a good day, I will not get super-soakered. The chemicals I bring with me cannot finish the job, though they are very strong and evil. Why does Mr. Zuckerberg insist on dispensing maple syrup out of a beer keg? That is not its proper function. Still, the children of Facebook are kind to me. They do not make me clean the hot tub, though the fish, they are dead.

dark side of the book

Don't be fooled by Facebook's buttoned-down layout and computer-savvy HTML code. At the center of the main server farm sit a winking strumpet and a brooding hunk. The only thing blue about the Book is everything.

BLUE LAWS:
THE SIX THINGS YOU CAN'T DO ON THE BOOK

Laissez-faire as they are, Team Facebook does have boundaries.

No l33t-speak profanities, e.g., b00bs, p3nis, nutzzz.

No status messages that ref a San Diego Necklace or a Philadelphia Tuba.

No faux lesbian-ism (it demeans genuine Sapphic love).

"Cock-n-balls" may only refer to the British beef-based pastry.

No X-rated anagrams to evade Rule 1, e.g., 00bbs, cr0tums.

If one of your Favorite Movies is Deep Throat, *it must be for the his-torical allusion.*

"GROUP" SEX

This was in college.

I'd heard a rumor about a group sex scene, but I never really believed it. Wishful thinking, I figured, no different than nano-technology or Tobey Maguire. Sure, there was the annual naked jamboree sponsored by the High Energy Physics Club. But an entryway orgy? Unlikely.

But one day I got this odd Facebook message. "You're cute. Want in?" was all it read. A girl in my psych section had sent it. You know the type: all cigarettes and hair. Attractive in that librarian-gone-wild way, the kind you want to "check out."

What did she mean? I messaged her back: "Yes, I'm in, as long as it isn't illegal or affiliated with the Medieval Club." Those guys really shouldn't be allowed to use authentic battle-axes.

The next day, I received an invitation to join the group "Fidelio." Seemed innocuous enough, as that's not one of Beethoven's more erotic works. But the members were tan and into R. Crumb: just the kind of people you'd expect to be part of a group sex scene. Also, they all listed "group sex" under Activities.

They welcomed me with some grooming advice. "Lose the Van Dyck." "Triceps before biceps." "Tan until pecan." They also recommended I give electronica a chance, which I had been meaning to do for a while anyway.

I didn't hear anything for a few days. Then I got this Facebook invite from the psych-section girl: "Wigglesworth H-11. Saturday. Midnight. Bring a trendy energy beverage." I felt more excited than a bar mitzvah boy in a brothel. This would be my D-Day.

Unfortunately, I hadn't been checking my Facebook account regularly, so I only got the message on Sunday. Never heard from any of 'em again and was kicked out of the group. The moral of this story is pretty obvious re: logging onto your Facebook account at least once a day.

But Facebook is so young, you say, what knows it of death? Alas, in Web 2.0 years, the Book has already attained crotchety middle age, and that tightness in its left shoulder is likely not the result of a lunch-hour keg-stand.

DEATHS CAUSED BY THE BOOK

To date, there is only one death directly attributable to Facebook. The circumstances of the case are chilling, but it contains a useful lesson about Book etiquette. Keep in mind the following story is entirely made up . . . of facts.

Tanya and Sara were BFFs. Which was great. But Tanya had a secret. Her father was the Number Two guy in the Russian mob—in charge of all counterfeit Fabergé eggs. And he made a powerful enemy when he tried to pass off herring roe as caviar to a fellow Don. On the Don's birthday.

Long story short, a contract was taken out against Tanya's life—a custom reserved only for egregious slights and humdrum Wednesdays. But when the bumbling hitman misplaced the file photo, he turned to Facebook for help. Unfortunately, Tanya had one of those Siamese Profile Pics (you know the kind, two girls press their cheeks together and match grins.) Which was Tanya and which her innocent friend Sara? Impossible to say for sure. With no time to spare, the hitman eeny-meeny-miny-moe'd the pic . . . and he moe'd wrong.

There's a happy ending, however. Sara's ghost went on to success-fully terrorize white-collar criminals in the greater Chicago area.

SIAMESE PROFILE PIC

DEATHS ON THE BOOK

What happens when someone on the Book dies? We asked the Facebook Mortician, Gary.

Q. *So, what does happen when someone on the Book dies?*

A. Their gifts go to their top friends. As determined randomly.

Q. *That's kind of morbid.*

A. Oh, please. If you die on LinkedIn, they give away your LinkPoints to strangers.

Q. *Huh.*

A. And you don't want to know about death on Friendster.

Q. *Umm—*

A. They sell the content of your profile to McSweeney's.

Q. *Wow.*

A. The worst is MySpace, of course. . . . Ever wonder where medical texts get their stock photos?

Q. *Is that even possible?*

A. Take a look at this:

Health and Homework

Congregations tend to condemn whatever Wired *praised six months earlier. Hence, Facebook was mentioned frequently at pulpits around the world in December 2007.*

"Our children are spending too much time looking at the Facebook when they should be looking at the Holy Book. Stalking their friends, when they should be stalking the devil. Uploading photos when they should be uploading their soul onto God's hard drive. The Lord has a gigabyte reserved for each and every one of his children."

"God has a Facebook. Uh-huh. Amen. It's right there on his brand new Mac (top-of-the-line, 'cuz He's God.) And what does God do on His Facebook? Same things you do when you go on your Facebook. Poke around, check up on sinners, judge. Except when God friends you, it turns you into an angel, and you can jump about 50 percent higher."

"Devil's got a Facebook, too. It's called MySpace."

"It is written in the Kabbalah that all books are sacred objects. Which raises the question: is Facebook a book? Grand Rabbi Uziel writes, 'Yeah, sure, why not, I mean its second syllable is book.' On the other hand, Chief Rabbi Abramovitz counters, 'You've got to be kidding me, whoever heard of a book that's 35 million pages long? And I don't mean the latest Pynchon!'"

"Fact: If you think a website can clear your dianetics, you're a couple emgrams short. Fact: L.R.H. has more thetans than Facebook has members. Fact: Buy T.C. in *MI:3* on DVD."

"Fire! Brimstone! Ash! Monkeys!
Goats! Slobbering dogs! Vivisection!
Damnation! Friend Whores!"

Facebook has already minted more paper millionaires than an Albanian investment fund. And they haven't even rolled out the Poke Tax.

SCAMS

The Spanish Profile: "Natalie Portman" offers you friendship if you do her series of small favors, including buying lots of bootleg *Star Wars* DVDs on Facebook Marketplace and listing Keira Knightley as your least favorite actress.

FAUX NATALIE PORTMAN

The Mark Zuckerfraud: "Zuckerberg" offers to let you be CEO for a day if you'll just tell him your checking account number and ATM pin. After you divulge the info, the fraudster puts you in charge of Face Booked Corp., a privately owned prison.

Gifts: Facebook Gifts.

The Bait-and-Snitch: A high-school student offers you money to buy him beer. After you agree, he blackmails you by tagging you in unspeakable photos until you agree to buy him the beer for free. In the end, you share a six-pack in a parking lot and talk about life. **Gifts:** Facebook Gifts.

Six Degrees of Degradation: A person with your last name and similar features claims to be a lost relative. He or she appeals to your sense of family pride and asks for some money to go to law school. But the name is fake, the pic photoshopped, and the law school actually a stripper academy.

Nigerian Scam, Book-style: Like the popular e-mail scam, except using Facebook messages. The son of a deposed African dictator offers you a chunk of his spoils if you'll pay the transaction costs. Watch out for Nigerians who are in the Bangkok network.

HOW MUCH IS FACEBOOK REALLY WORTH?

We asked the Zuck himself:

"The only thing that's worth anything is friendship. Now get out of my mansions."

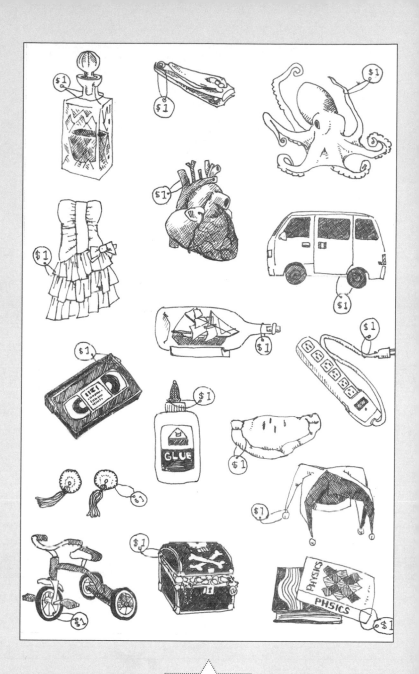

GIFTS

the
future of
facebook

"WHAT SHALL BE AND MUST BE IS THE GROUND OF THAT WHICH IS [FACEBOOK]." — *Friedrich Nietzsche*

A FUTURE SO BRIGHT IT CAN ONLY BE
REPRESENTED ON THE KINDLE EDITION

The future of Facebook is bright—bright as a thousand blue suns. Will it take over the Internet itself? Only time, and maybe Richard Branson, can tell. Worst-case scenario, it takes over half the Internet and all of Denmark. More likely, Facebook messages replace e-mail entirely, and the New York Times *becomes an optional daily wall post. In the meantime, here is exactly what the future of Facebook will look like (as refracted through our brains):*

3-D PROFILES

3-D is intrinsically better than 2-D. Every 3-D movie is better than every 2-D movie. Every sculpture is better than every painting. Cardboard is better than paper.

What will a 3-D profile be like? Besides (obviously) amazing.

You are in a room. One wall of this room has pictures of all your friends. It's quite long. It's like a Great Wall of China for friends, but built with a minimum of slave labor. Wall posts, though, are no longer written on a wall; they appear in thin air via laser-beam. (They are still called wall posts.) Your gifts will be stored

in a giant or tiny toy chest, depending. It has a lock, and the key is hidden underneath your frenemy rug. Photo albums look like regular photo albums, but the people in them are actually dancing.

You activate apps by opening a door and navigating an elaborate maze. The maze is a coding error.

Also, your profile pic is now a statue of you standing in a fountain.

FACEBOOK FOR DOGS

There's already an app that allows dogs to join Facebook. It's pretty good, but it relegates dogs to a second-class status on the Book. With the rise in status of both Facebook and dogs in the coming years, the Team will create a DogBook proper.

DogBook will be nothing like regular Facebook, design-wise. What does a dog care for a sharp, minimalist aesthetic or words? Food, friendship, and fun, that's all a dog wants; cats, carcinogens, and celery, that's all a dog abhors.

More than three-quarters of the page is a picture of the dog. It's typically an action shot—catching a Frisbee in its mouth and an Aerobie with its tail on a trampoline, for example. The rest is comprised of pictures of a) doggie friends; b) cool humans; and c) dinosaurs (with whom dogs used to hang out). Some humans who don't like to read will join DogBook and carve out a niche of their own.

What about CatBook?

Well, what about it?

FACEBOOK UNIVERSITY

Mark Zuckerberg will one day decide to return to Harvard to complete his degree. For the duration of his stay, everyone calls it Facebook University. He rides around Cambridge in a coach drawn by distinguished Derby winners and wears a top hat of solid ivory. He pays professors to write his papers in the courses of lesser professors. None of his classes begin until he sits down, and no class ends until he gets up. For his seminar in Facebook studies, however, everything he writes is automatically correct, since the class is about what's inside his brain. In the dining hall, he is permitted to eat the dinner menu for lunch. His laundry is done by a trained cobbler. He is allowed to keep any book from the library for as long as he likes or until his loan expires, whichever comes first. When he finally graduates, a monkey in a mortarboard picks up his diploma so that he may sleep in.

FACEBOOK BUCKS

Like Disney World, *Second Life*, and Canada, Facebook will one day decide it needs its own proprietary form of currency, called Facebook Bucks, only useful for making wagers on the Friendship Stock Exchange. "What is such a thing?" you ask. It is a system for making wagers on what your friends do in a given period of time (as verified by changes on their profiles). So, for example, you can bet whether or not your friend Parker breaks up with his girlfriend by March. It's not gambling, because Facebook Bucks are literally worthless. You won't even be allowed to use them to buy Facebook Gifts.

RETRO FACEBOOK

Facebook is already complex, and it's only getting more so.

Recall that Facebook began its life as a zen rock garden. It was what it didn't have (vids, crazy fonts, old people) that made it good. However, its middle age will resemble Times Square on New Year's Eve, with several more helicopters and a petting zoo. Hey, we all gotta pay the bills.

A few Booksters will hearken to a simpler time. Some will self-consciously remove all apps, avoid posting to walls, and, in extreme cases, delete their gifts. They will be camping out in Central Park. And it will be nice and fine, and their maximalist friends will admire them the way the rest of us admire people who genuinely don't like reality television.

But for a few, that will not be enough. Remember the kids who, with the advent of *Wolfenstein 3-D*, still preferred the text-based adventures of *Zork*? Kids with imaginations so sophisticated they didn't want graphics, as that might explode their brains? These are not merely vegans but full-blown, broom-sweeping Mennonites. They will forge a text-based Facebook.

It will look something like this:

facebook

I am wearing my
J-Hop hoodie and
giving the sign of
the "V." There are
kegs fore and aft.
Is that Max D. in
the background? You
can't quite tell.

<profile> Hi, I'm
Dustin. Let's see, I
guess I should tell
you about some of
my favorite movies
first. Well, the last
thing I saw on DVD
was Donnie Darko for
my existentialism
class, and it was
surprisingly good,

even if it wasn't a Blu-Ray. I've been listening to a lot of Christmas music lately.

<friends>
Max Delano
Harrison Potemkin
Sara Slaughter
Sara S. Borealis

HOW WILL FACEBOOK TAKE ON GOOGLE?

Through a series of extravagant sporting matches.

Global Capture the Flag: The prime meridian divides the two sides. The flags are the Hope Diamond and the Millennium Diamond, respectively. You tag a person by grabbing smartly the lapels of his or her sport coat. All forms of transportation are permitted, and aerofoils are especially encouraged. The jails

HUMAN STRATEGO

are luxury yachts equipped with celebrity chefs. Stonehenge is a designated no-man's land. The winning team gets a parade in the parking lot of their choice.

Race to the Moon: Get to the moon first using just the parts found in NASA's garage. Get back too, if you want a prize.

Human Stratego: The classic board game played with real armies on a big field. The guns are fake, but the knives are real.

AGE-APPROPRIATE MODIFICATIONS

As the population of Facebook ages, profile fields will have to adjust. Some changes anticipated by 2060:

Favorite Movies will become Favorite Medications.
Favorite Books will become Favorite Great-Grandchildren.
Favorite Quote will become Epitaph.

FACEBOOK ON TV

A lot of people will try to cash in on the whole Facebook thing through the medium of television.

The Chronicles of Facebook (*reality show*): Purported to be a Real World-ish exploration of life at Camp Facebook, it is actually filmed at the offices of Yahoo! Mash, a fact that would be revealed in the final episode via a message in some mashed potatoes. Never got there, though. *5 episodes*

The Chris Muskovitz Show (*talk show*): The Team Facebook billionaire buys himself a talk show complete with desk, couch, and Andy Richter. Instead of live guests, he chats with his friends online and they make snarky comments about nonbillionaires. Never really finds its niche on the CW. *3 episodes*

The News Feed (*news show*): Headlines from the world of Facebook. The most popular segment is Awesome Profile of the Day, until a blogger discovers they're all relatives and friends of the producers. *18 episodes*

CHRIS HANSEN

To Catch a Fauxfile (*investigative journalism*): Spin-off of the popular but controversial *To Catch a Predator*. Chris Hansen entraps the masterminds behind celebrity fauxfiles with the promise of frozen drinks. The show runs into trouble when it's revealed Hansen has become a total Facebook addict, to the neglect of his family and offline friends. *9 episodes*

Intervention: Facebook Addiction (*hard-hitting reality show*): One-off of the *Intervention* series. Relatives and therapists attempt to treat Chris Hansen for his Book addiction. In the final minutes, Hansen breaks down and begs a laptop for his soul back. Guest appearances by recovering Book addicts Anderson Cooper and Imogen Heap. *1 episode*

The Code of Love (*sitcom*): A lonely Seattle-based programmer makes an app that finds one's Facebook soul mate. Unfortunately, it works for everyone but him, so he moves back in with his parents, a retired cop with accrued wisdom and a meddlesome mom with a heart of dignity. *105 episodes*

SCHOLARLY PAPERS THAT WILL
BE WRITTEN ABOUT THE BOOK

WHY FACEBOOK?
WHY NOT?

*A Study on the Arbitrariness
of Success in the Internet Age
of Stupidity*

YALE PRESS

WHAT IS THIS
FACEBOOK
THING, ANYWAY?

*A Warm Introduction to
Facebook for Poets and
Gentleman Scholars*

MIT PRESS

BLUE IS
THE BLANDEST
COLOR

*How Facebook Succeeded
Through Unobtrusiveness
and Okay-ness*

MIT PRESS

FACEBOOK
**is Kind of the Worst
Thing . . . for Stupid
People:** *How Facebook is
Actually a Great Thing for
Smart People*

YALE PRESS

GOD WOULDN'T
JOIN FACEBOOK,
&
NEITHER SHOULD
A YALIE

YALE PRESS

FACEBOOK IS
THE MOST
OVERRATED
WEBSITE EVER

a bibliography

YALE PRESS

TARGETED ADS

Team Facebook will try a lot of ideas to make money off their quirky website. This is the best one.

An algorithm will "read" your profile pic and show you a relevant ad.

If you have/are . . .	you'll get an ad for . . .
no pants on	Dockers
a shaved head	scalp shampoo
an ironic moustache	a spittoon
a hemp necklace	a hemp tuxedo
facial piercings and feathers in your hair	Oberlin College
money literally bursting out of your pockets	clown pants
just chilling out	sweatpants
eating a burrito	Bob's Burrito Brothel
in a swamp	swamp insurance
kicking a soccer ball	Europe
drinking out of a trophy cup	Queen's "We are the Champions" (MP3)
sleeping	sleepy juice (alcohol)

COMPANIES FACEBOOK WILL BUY OUT

- find-a-friend-4-a-dollar
- alumni groper
- keep-in-touchster
- stay-in-touch_bot
- touch-your-friends@the_Internet
- he-mail
- phriend-phisher
- APPle sauce
- the New York Mets

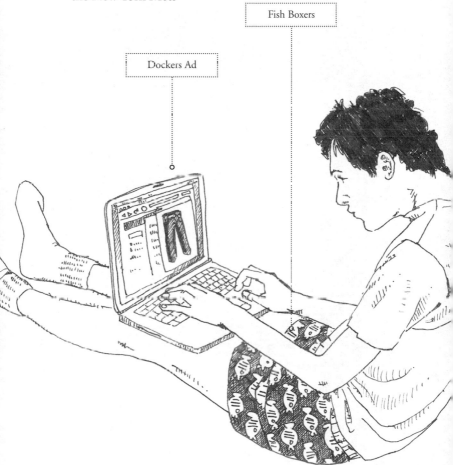

Fish Boxers

Dockers Ad

Congratulations on your . . .

free
facebook
gift

you can redeem it on the web

Just go to:

http://www.thefacebookbook.com/free_gift/facebook_book_
free_gift_2k8/first_edition/limited_edition/wrapping_paper/
box/inner_box/more_wrapping_paper/bows_and_rib-
bons/facebook_book_free_gift_2k8_edition/another_box/
the_gift_itself/the_facebook_book_free_gift_absolutely_free/
free_gift_disclaimer/there_is_nothing_to_disclaim/free_
gift_2k8/expires_never/box/small_box/wrapping_paper_
again/final_box/last_inner_box/one_last_string/open_box/
box_opened/innermost_part_of_the_package/Abrams_ logo/
Abrams_ crest/Abrams_scal/facebook_logo/facebook_crest/fa-
cebook_minor_crest/facebook_box/empty_box/next_box/box/
wrapping_paper_yet_again/box/inner_box/more_wrapping_
paper/bows_and_ribbons/facebook free gift 2k8 edition_
gift_second_box/secondary_inner_box/tertiary_inner_box/
more_wrapping_paper/facebook_logo_and_crest_and_seal/
and_minor_seal/inner_box/secondary_inner_box/ribbons_
and_bow/trimmings/something_that_looks_like_trimmings/
tight_wrapping_paper/scissors/shreds_of_wrapping_paper/
super_secret_inner_box/rope/yet_another_box/leftover_wrap-
ping_paper_from_last_Christmas/twine/brown_paper/box/
butcher_paper/box/another_box/shoelaces/old_newspa-
per_funnies_from_1997/really_now_the_last_bit_of_pack-
ing/scotch_tape/box/Styrofoam_peanuts/inner_box/
bubble_wrap/little_facebook_blue_box/tissue_paper/gauze/

gift.gif

Again, congratulations.

**Answers to Wall Post vs.
Message Quiz:** You should
probably never say any of
those things to anyone.

facebook
glossary
{not in alphabetical order}

Facebook
The thing itself; *res ipsa*; the object of our labors and succor of our days; that to which nature in all her majesty tends; the universe in miniature; a website.

Bookster
A user of Facebook, as in "If you're not a Bookster by now, you probably still have a Discman in your Trapper Keeper."

profile
The fundamental unit of Facebook; without profiles, Facebook would be naught but a collection of Yahoo!-grade webgames and soggy banner ads.

friend
In the binary world of Facebook, friend is 1; collect all of these and win.

fauxfile
A fake profile that was not created by its subject; often it's for a celebrity, but sometimes for a fictional character, such as Jack Black.

snowfile
A profile with a lot of white space (i.e., snow); these are maintained by the kind of kids who wear turtlenecks.

showfile

A really showy profile, like if Mel Brooks were putting on a musical, except it was a Facebook profile; a MySpace-y Facebook profile.

pro-file

An expertly made profile; you read it and think, "Damn, I'd like to befriend that fellow . . . or at least learn from him."

glowfile

A profile that is illuminated with the glow of human warmth; it evokes a fireplace in your childhood home, mom's cooking, a time before Facebook.

roverfile

A profile for a dog, not limited to Rovers.

nofile

It got deleted.

gift

A matrix of colored pixels arranged to resemble a novelty item; its cost on the open market is 99 cents, and despite a popular belief to the contrary, only 0.00 percent of the proceeds go to charity.

app
A gaming cartridge for your profile, more or less.

 Camp Facebook
The headquarters of the Facebook Corp., located in sunny Palo Alto, California, across the street from an In-N-Out Burger and the Ron Jon Surf Shop.

 Team Facebook
The Facebook workforce; they are a team in the sense that they excel at Nerf sports and computer programming.

 photo album
A little slice of Flickr right on Facebook; the net's largest repository of documented wine-tasting parties.

 fauxto album
An album where the photos are photoshopped or, in a rare case, highly photorealistic drawings of Marc Brainerd skeet-shooting.

 network
The village you call home in the big blue world of Facebook; come back here after a late night of pokendipity and sing dirges with the clan into the dawn.

 poke
To prod another Bookster with a virtual finger, classily.

pokendipity P
Poking random people outside of your network on the off-chance this will start a human relationship; poking with John Cusack's finger.

frenemy F
A Facebook friend who is in fact your rival; your Facebook friendship is the Internet equivalent of binding together the left hands of knife-fighters.

enemiend E
A friend in the real world who is a rival on Facebook (e.g., in terms of Scrabulous high scores).

floater F
A friend in your collection who's presence is a mystery; you might allow him to linger on the off chance he becomes the next Ron Paul.

Facebook video F
Facebook's answer to YouTube; YouTube responded with FriendTV, five webisodes about some pals who team up in the happening part of Chicago town.

Facebook Markup Language F
A "language" used by the Team to create the magic; sounds like Portuguese spoken by a Croat.

Facebook Blue
Midway between teal and the color of sadness; the hue of Mark Zuckerberg's eyes on a rainy day.

social networking site
A place on the Web to just be yourself—a star.

Facebook Marketplace
A Craigslist that permits the sale of friendship.

status
was procrastinating inside-joke sleep guilty chocolate hookup.

events
Happenings; shindigs; sit-abouts; keggers; bashes; parades; caucuses; street fun; any kind of thing really as long as it benefits the environment.

groups
The underappreciated jewel of the Book; you know those humorous T-shirts that reference *Little Miss Sunshine* or New Jersey's inherent satanism? These are those T-shirts for your profile.

ACKNOWLEDGMENTS AND POKES

Designer: **Alissa Faden**

Art Director: **Galen Smith**

Production Manager: **Jacquie Poirier**

Another Production Dude: **MacAdam Smith**

Facebook Muse: **Maxine Kaplan**

Guy who like basically wrote the book: **Eric Klopfer**

Promoter: **Kerry Liebling**

Less Scrupulous Promoter: **Maggie Maggio**

Capo di Tutti Capi: **Aiah Wieder**

Special Thanks: **Michael Jacobs, Eric Himmel, Leslie Stoker, Jennifer Brunn, Julia Coblentz, Andrew Blauner, Maud Bryt, Caroline Miller, Marie Morris, Simon Rich, and the Internet itself.**